From Riches to a Ruin

From Riches to a Ruin

The Arkwrights of Sutton Scarsdale Hall

Paul Halksworth

First published in Great Britain in 2019 by

Bannister Publications Ltd
118 Saltergate
Chesterfield
Derbyshire S40 1NG

Copyright © Paul Halksworth

ISBN 978-1-909813-56-4

Paul Halksworth asserts the moral right to be identified
as the author of this work

A catalogue record for this book is available from the British Library

This book is sold subject to the condition that it shall not, by way of trade or otherwise, be lent, re-sold, hired out or otherwise circulated without the copyright holder's prior consent in any form of binding or cover other than that in which it is published and without a similar condition including this condition being imposed on the subsequent purchase.

All rights reserved. No part of this book may be reproduced or transmitted in any form or by any means, electronic or mechanical including photocopying, recording or by any information storage and retrieval system, without permission from the copyright holder, in writing.

Typeset in Sabon by Escritor Design, Bournemouth

Printed and bound in Great Britain

This book is dedicated to my wife Sandra, daughter Susie and son Daniel for their wonderful support.

Without their help and patience this book would never have been completed.

Contents

The Arkwright Family Tree ------------------------------------- ix
Preface--1
Introduction--5
1. The Establishment of a Dynasty--------------------------9
2. The Hall and its Occupants before the Arkwrights- 15
3. Robert and Frances: Marriage and Social Life-------25
4. Life at the Hall---39
5. Major William Arkwright -------------------------------45
6. Godfrey Harry Arkwright-------------------------------49
7. William Arkwright (The Younger)----------------------51
8. Social and Economic Development on
   The Sutton Scarsdale Estate---------------------------------61
9. Sutton Rock--73
10. The 1919 Sale---85
11. Conclusion--91
Epilogue---103
Bibliography---105
Acknowledgements--109
Photographs---111

```
Patience Holt (1)  =  Sir Richard Arkwright  =  Margaret Biggens (2)
   (d.1756)            (1732-1792)                (1723-1811)
      │
      └──── Richard Arkwright = Mary Simpson
                (1755-1843)      (1755-1827)
                      │
   ┌──────────────┬───────────┬──────────────┐
Elizabeth      Richard      * Robert         Peter
(1780-1838)   (1781-1832)  (1783-1857)    (1784-1866)
                                =
                       Frances Crawford Kemble
                            (c.1785-1849)
                                │
        ┌───────────────┬───────────────┐
     Charles         George          William
   (1806-1808)    (1807-1856)     (1809-1859)
                                      =
                            Fanny Susan Thornwell
                               (c.1833-1911)
                                      │
   ┌──────────────┬───────────────┬──────────────┐
Fanny Elizabeth   Emma         Sophia         * William
(1853-1912)   (1854-1877)   (1855-1941)     (1857-1925)
                                                 =
                                    Agnes Mary Somers-Cocks
                                         (1859-1940)

                                           (No issue)
```

The Arkwright Family Tree
(Simplified to the Sutton Scarsdale Branch)

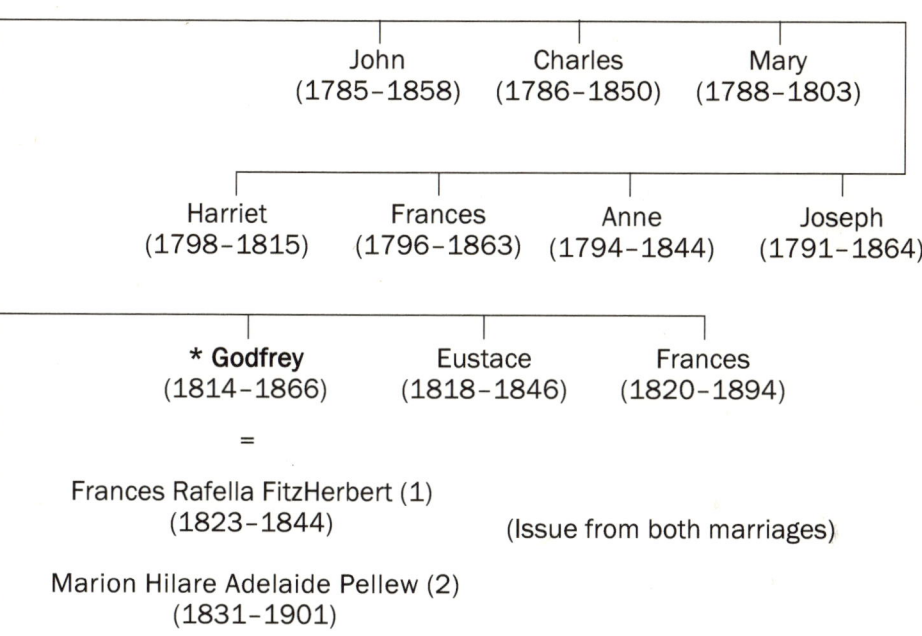

```
              John           Charles          Mary
          (1785-1858)     (1786-1850)     (1788-1803)

    Harriet        Frances         Anne           Joseph
  (1798-1815)   (1796-1863)   (1794-1844)     (1791-1864)

       * Godfrey         Eustace         Frances
      (1814-1866)     (1818-1846)     (1820-1894)
           =
Frances Rafella FitzHerbert (1)
       (1823-1844)                (Issue from both marriages)

Marion Hilare Adelaide Pellew (2)
       (1831-1901)
```

* Owners of the Sutton Scarsdale Estate

Preface

Just north of Junction 29 on the M1 motorway through Derbyshire, two great houses face each other across the Vale of Scarsdale. Situated on the edge of the scarp slope of the Vale is Bolsover Castle: built of limestone and sandstone it was designed by Robert Smythson for Bess of Hardwick's son Sir Charles Cavendish; it then passed to his son, Sir William, an expert horse rider who later became the Duke of Newcastle. Bolsover Castle was originally constructed in the early seventeenth century upon the ruins of a Norman motte and bailey castle then later enlarged and extended by John, Smythson's son. Directly opposite the castle and across the Vale, at the summit of a gentle, grassy slope stands Sutton Scarsdale Hall, known locally as Sutton Hall: it was built in the early eighteenth century by Francis Smith of Warwick for Nicholas Leake, the 4th Earl of Scarsdale.

Both buildings are now in the care of English Heritage but the contrast between them could not be greater. Bolsover Castle is roofed, its rooms, containing intriguing paintings, are richly decorated and its magnificent 'riding house' is world famous: it is also the subject of a book, *Cavalier*, by Lucy Worsley. It stands on the same side of the valley as the old and new Hardwick Halls which are a short distance away. Sutton Scarsdale Hall stands today as a roofless, picturesque, evocative shell; it lies at the edge of a small country village, isolated from the majority of country house visitors yet visible from the motorway along which thousands travel each day. It was once the grandest mansion of its date in Derbyshire according to Nicholas Pevsner, even rivalling Chatsworth House, and a home to three great families between 1728 and 1919 – the Leakes, Clarkes and Arkwrights. To the south of the Hall and bordering the Sutton Scarsdale estate stood Oldcotes, the last mansion built by Bess of Hardwick for her second son William, Earl of Devonshire. It was completed by 1599 but after demolition it is now a private working farm.

My interest in the Arkwrights of Sutton Scarsdale has quite complex origins: I was born in the parish of Sutton-cum-Duckmanton and christened in St Mary's Church adjoining the Hall, where my parents had married during World War Two. After my father's demobilisation from the Royal Navy in 1946 we would walk to 'Sutton ponds', which remained then as remnants of the once great estate and before opencasting destroyed them. Whilst at junior school in the nearby village of Calow (to where we had moved when I was six years old) myself and another boy visited, on several occasions, a house called Sutton Rock, because a friend in our class lived there. The house had originally been built by the Arkwrights and it stood on gently sloping land accessed down Rock Lane and a short distance from the Hall's drive entrance. Then as a teenager I occasionally wandered with friends through the overgrown, unevenly floored, tree-choked shell of the Hall, completely ignorant of its origins, history and links with the Arkwright family.

After a 12-year career as a design engineer I attended Manchester Polytechnic (now Manchester Metropolitan University) and then the University of Nottingham, becoming a history teacher in Nottinghamshire before moving to teach in Derbyshire. One of my tutors in Manchester was Dr Robert (Bob) Fitton, co-author with A. P. Wadsworth of '*The Strutts and the Arkwrights*', and author of the classic '*The Arkwrights, Spinners of Fortune*', and it was he who sparked my interest in the economic and social history of Derbyshire, particularly that of Cromford, associated with Sir Richard Arkwright. I wrote my school's GCSE coursework relating to the development of the Cromford Mills and village, and, with other staff, took pupils each year on field trips to the area. Now retired, I am a member of the Arkwright Society, a former guide at the Mills and I conduct tours of Sutton Scarsdale Hall for the Society as part of the Heritage Open Days, as well as for various other organisations and history groups, all in conjunction with English Heritage. Sutton Scarsdale Hall and the Arkwrights who lived there for almost a hundred years are therefore the inspiration for this book.

I have attempted to tell the story of the Arkwright ownership of the Sutton Scarsdale estate while also detailing the origins and architectural development of the Hall. Staff of the Chatsworth House Archives, the

Derbyshire Public Records Office at Matlock and the Chesterfield Local History Library have all been very helpful and supportive, while many individuals have been an enthusiastic, constant and reliable source of information. I hope, also, that this book fulfils the wish that the late, local historian Pamela Kettle had of writing a history of the Sutton Scarsdale branch of the Arkwright family as a complement to other local history books that she had written.

My aim has always been that this book will provide a sound base of information which will benefit the Arkwright Society as well as various history groups, the local community and many individuals, including those who have viewed the Hall with interest, either from the M1 motorway or from a more intimate distance.

I have researched books, articles, documents, memoirs, maps and photographs, all of which have contributed to my knowledge and writing where some authors have been quoted in the text. I hope that their work has been reflected accurately in my account and I also hope that this book will encourage further study, research and writing.

Introduction

Robert and Frances Arkwright took over the Sutton Scarsdale Estate, probably in early 1837, moving their growing family from Stoke Hall to Sutton Scarsdale Hall. It was the beginning of a 'Golden Age' of farming which lasted until the 1870s and which saw national improvements introduced throughout the country.

The Corn Laws, introduced in 1815 when the war against Napoleon ended stated that if the price of home-produced wheat in Britain reached 80s. (£4) a quarter then foreign wheat could be imported. The Corn Laws allowed land owners and farmers – the largest group in parliament – to protect their profits as well as being against foreign competition because they feared that the import of foreign wheat would cause the price to fall: during the French wars farmers had sold home-produced wheat for very high prices.

So when Robert Arkwright took over the Sutton Scarsdale Estate the price of bread was being kept artificially high and the poor suffered great hardship. Farming still flourished between 1847 and 1870 because foreign competition was not as strong as farmers and landowners feared: sea transport was not advanced enough to allow imports from the Americas or Australia and British farming was efficient and productive. The years 1840-75 particularly saw farming succeed; an increasing population, particularly in the towns, provided a lucrative market because of the increased demand for farm produce, and the production of meat, butter and cheese rose rapidly.

Helped by quicker transport – a result of the Industrial Revolution of 1760-1830 – farming was efficient and production rose by about 70% in this period of 'High Farming'. Robert Arkwright's ownership of the Sutton Scarsdale Estate saw great technical advance, steadily increasing profits and a rising standard of living among nearly all classes which included estate farmers who had the home market virtually to themselves;

it was a period of great agricultural prosperity.

During this time the importance of the Derbyshire dairy trade increased and product prices rose from the 1840s. The arrival of the Midland Railway provided a new outlet for the dairy industry in the form of the liquid milk trade which, by the turn of the century had expanded so fast that, as well as saving livestock and dairy farming from total collapse, it had superseded the important cheese-making industry. The expansion of population brought about by the Industrial Revolution created a large demand for liquid milk which could be sold to nearby urban markets and transported by the new railways directly, for example, to Sheffield and London. Large dairies such as the Express Dairy at Rowsley near Bakewell provided collecting points for the marketing of milk provided by many small farmers, including those on the Sutton Scarsdale Estate.

The Corn Laws were abolished in 1846, after the Anti-Corn Law League, which had its headquarters in Manchester, had been formed in 1839 by representatives of the manufacturing and commercial classes reflecting the increasing power of industrialists over aristocratic and gentry landowners: the rising industrial classes of the towns had gained much more influence in Parliament and they challenged the declining landowning gentry. The 1845 Irish famine and an increasing belief in free trade also contributed to the abolition of the Corn Laws. The Liberal Party, together with part of the Tory Party, voted for repeal.

Robert died in 1859 leaving the Sutton Scarsdale Estate to his only surviving son, Godfrey, who died in 1866. William, the only son of Major William Arkwright inherited the estate which was run by trustees until William came of age.

The later part of the 19th century would see massive changes, not just in agriculture but in the economy as a whole. The 'Golden Age' of farming was followed by the 'Great Depression' (usually dated 1873-96), which brought problems for the owners of landed estates which included the Arkwrights of Sutton Scarsdale: William suffered financial problems throughout his ownership. The period of farming depression was the result of the combination of several factors which made farming increasingly difficult, bringing the prosperous years to an end in the mid-1870s. Lengthy periods of appalling weather over the three decades from the 1870s, beginning with five unusually bad successive summers from 1873 to 1877, ruined crops and rotted livestock, culminating in a serious outbreak of foot and mouth disease in 1883, bringing an end to the prosperous years. Loans, repayable over a 25-year period, had been made available from the 1850s, leaving landowners owing large sums.

The real problem for British farmers was increasing competition from abroad, resulting in North American grain and cheap refrigerated lamb from Australia and New Zealand as well as beef from South America flooding European markets because of great agricultural expansion and improved sea transport. With the gradual increasing import of cheap grain after the abolition of the Corn Laws the acreage under wheat dropped sharply in Britain. With unemployment rising and wages falling, agricultural labourers sought work in towns, some of them forced to become general labourers because of their redundancy from agriculture, or they attempted to 'better' themselves: some emigrated overseas. Between 1870 and 1914 the number of workers on the land fell from 1¼ million to well below 1 million while the overall population rose by about 40% in the same period. However, the depression of the late 19th century was very uneven in its effect; farm incomes must have fallen nearly everywhere in monetary terms and the depression was worst in the heavy soils of southern England. Gladwyn Turbutt, in his 'History of Derbyshire', has indicated that Derbyshire was hit less hard than some other counties because of its greater dependence on dairy farming: the liquid milk trade saved many Derbyshire farmers from bankruptcy.

In Derbyshire in the Edwardian era 92% of farm land was tenanted and the average size of a holding was 42.2 acres, a situation which had hardly changed for over a century. The Sutton Scarsdale Estate fell into this category; many families on the estate had tenanted the same farms down the generations, reflecting the wider situation in Derbyshire.

The pre-eminence of agriculture amongst British industries had ended, although in Derbyshire and some areas of the Midlands and the North farmers producing milk or meat probably suffered no decrease in their economic position. The late 19th century was the period of large-scale rural decline in England and the time, too, when the social position of the landowners was first seriously undermined: the landlord class as a whole had suffered a permanent loss of capital and income. Between the 1870s and 1914 agriculture as a source of employment and means of livelihood greatly declined: in terms of net output it was more or less stagnating while most other large industries were still growing. Estate owners were faced with reduced rents generally from the 1880s, but also by the effects of capital taxation and death duties.

With the loss of wealth and the decline of social influence and political power as well as an inability to resist policies which ensured that the landowners' position would never be restored, only the tenant farmers came near to maintaining both their numbers and their incomes. The second and third Reform Acts of 1867 and 1884 gave a vote to a new political class who often resented the former influence of the landlord class. William Arkwright lived through this unsettling period from his 'coming of age' in 1878 to his sale of the whole estate in 1919. Despite government support during World War One agriculture slumped again soon after: the price of wheat halved and farmers were no longer guaranteed against losses.

The demise of the landed gentry and the dispersal of many of their estates ended a system based on manorial lordship which dated from the Norman Conquest. With the declining economic influence of agriculture, increasingly reduced by industrial and commercial wealth and with judicial power as magistrates no longer their exclusive preserve, the influence of the landed gentry largely disappeared, although their social prestige lasted until World War Two. Approximately 200 estates were sold before the beginning of World War One, with sales continuing throughout the war. In the three years after the end of World War One it is possible that a quarter of the land in England and Wales was sold. Sutton Scarsdale Hall and Wingerworth Hall are local examples of the decline of agriculture and landed gentry control and influence.

1

The Establishment of a Dynasty

At one o'clock on Thursday 18th November 1824, in London, various estates of Walter Butler, the deceased Marquis of Ormonde were offered for sale by auction. Created a Marquis in 1815 he had taken possession of the Sutton Scarsdale Estate by his marriage to the granddaughter and representative of Godfrey Bagnall Clarke. Mr George Robins, the auctioneer, was acting on behalf of the trustees of the late Marquis, who had died in August 1820, an act of Parliament and a decree of the Court of Chancery. The room at the Auction Mart was crowded with people, there to witness the sale of the Sutton Scarsdale estate as well as the Chilcote Estate which included the whole of a parish, the Brampton Estate which included mines of coal and ironstone as well as 2,450 acres of land and several dairy farms near Derby, Coventry and Newcastle-under-Lyme. The debts of the Marquis of Ormonde amounted to about £450,000 and they needed to be paid off as soon as possible as he had been paying nearly 10% interest on three-quarters of the debt as well as 5% interest for part of the debt. James, brother and heir of the Marquis was forced to sell the properties.

Both the *Morning Chronicle* of Friday 19th of November and the *Derby Mercury* of Wednesday 24th November carried very similar accounts of the auction. The sale of the greatest estate, that of Sutton Scarsdale, proceeded very briskly by £10,000 at a time until it reached £190,000. Then £195,000 was offered and there was a short pause. Mr Robins reminded everyone of the nobility of the Hall, the presence of stately elms and wide-spreading Spanish chestnuts. The bidding then rose immediately to £200,000 and a brief mention of the valuable mines of coal and ironstone on the estate as well as the Grecian architecture produced further bids up to £215,000. At this point there was a long pause and the whole room was breathless with expectation. Mr Robins declared that he could no longer detain the company. 'It cuts me to the heart, Gentlemen' he said, 'that it should go for such a trifle, but – at two hundred and fifteen thousand pounds once: at two hundred and fifteen thousand pounds twice, for the last time at two hundred and fifteen thousand pounds – for the very last time'. There was a further pause and someone banged his stick on the floor. The effect was electrical and a cry of 'gone' went up throughout the room. Mr Robins drew on all his experience and skill and at length order was restored; his eye glistened and with a shout of triumph he announced 'For two hundred and sixteen thousand; for your thousand pounds, a thousand thanks, Sir – for two hundred and sixteen thousand pounds [approximately £23 million today] for the very last time' and the hammer went down.

The purchaser, who had outbid the Duke of Devonshire's agent, was Richard Arkwright, son of Sir Richard, the cotton entrepreneur, and the Sutton Scarsdale estate was only one of several great estates bought by Richard, for his sons. The total amount produced by the sale of the Clarke estates was £315,800. Richard's own estimated value of the Sutton Scarsdale Estate had been £237,000. The estate of about 5,500 acres comprised, according to the sale document, 33 farms, 19 smallholdings, 70 dwelling houses, a licensed house, shops, cottages, accommodation, building land, Sutton Spring Wood and other woods as well as Sutton Scarsdale Hall which had beautiful gardens and a well-timbered deer park. Within the Hall's grounds were pleasure gardens containing, for example, an archery ground and croquet and tennis lawns, a kitchen garden, kennels, stabling, workshops and various other buildings.

Richard and his wife, Mary, had produced seven boys and five girls. Although three of the children died young – a boy before his first birthday and two of the girls in their teens – the remaining three daughters married into wealthy gentry and aristocratic families. Apart from buying several landed estates of various sizes in Derbyshire, Yorkshire and Cheshire (a policy that had not been pursued by his father), the younger Richard bought large estates for each of his surviving sons who inherited them at their father's death. The manor of Normanton Turville in Leicestershire, bought for £33,000 in 1796, became the home of Richard, his eldest son who died in 1832; it was then left to the Reverend Joseph, his youngest son; in 1809 Hampton Court in Herefordshire, costing £230,000, went to John. Several manors accompanying Mark Hall in Essex were acquired in 1819 at a cost of £100,000 on behalf of the Reverend Joseph, and in 1824 the Sutton Scarsdale estate was purchased for Robert. Finally, in 1826, Dunstall Hall in Staffordshire, at £42,000, was purchased for Charles who also inherited Skerne and Driffield in Yorkshire. Peter, the third son, lived at Rock House in Cromford after his grandfather Sir Richard's death, eventually inheriting Willersley Castle upon his father's death in 1843 as well as the Mellor and Marple Estate in Derbyshire and other landed interests in Lancashire and Cheshire.

The story of the creation of the Arkwright family's wealth has been well documented. Apart from Dr Fitton's classic account *'The Arkwrights, Spinners of Fortune'*, many books and pamphlets record the arrival in Cromford, Derbyshire, of Sir Richard Arkwright and his subsequent achievements. The Arkwright Society has done, and continues to do, sterling work in restoring and publicising the original site of the mills (now a World Heritage site as part of the Derwent Valley) that were built to house Arkwright's cotton-spinning machines. Built by Arkwright, John Kay and Thomas Highs after much experimentation, the original machine, called a 'Roller-Spinning Device' in Arkwright's patent description of 1769 became known as the 'Water Frame' after he relocated from his initial horse-powered Nottingham site to utilise the sough water and the Bonsall Brook at Cromford as power sources for his machines. After Arkwright's construction of the world's first water-powered cotton-spinning mill in 1771 Cromford became established as a thriving, independent community supported by his expanding cotton enterprise.

Richard Arkwright was knighted in 1786 and appointed High Sheriff of Derbyshire in 1787. At this time he commenced the building of Willersley Castle, designed by the architect William Thomas of London, and a house which no doubt Sir Richard felt would reflect his social standing. A fire which gutted the interior of the house delayed its building and in 1792, the year of its eventual completion, Sir Richard died. At his death he owned factories in Scotland, Manchester, Staffordshire and the Derwent Valley, including Cromford in Derbyshire, the site of his first cotton mill. His assets and cash were estimated at just under half a million pounds (over £200 million today).

Sir Richard's success had been due to his entrepreneurship as well as his inventiveness; through the use of technology which combined the newly developed cotton-spinning machinery with water as a power source, he introduced the world to a system of mass production. His opportunism determined financial and business sense, supportive but rigid and specific management of his workforce and complete single-minded control of his businesses made the system of production work. His motto, *Multa tuli fecique* (I have endured and done many things) was certainly appropriate.

Sir Richard had married twice: his first wife, Patience Holt, had given birth to Richard on 19th December 1755, but she died the following October and in March 1761, he married Margaret Biggens. She gave birth to Susannah in December of that year. Two more daughters, Ellen and Anne, died in infancy. At some stage Richard and Margaret became estranged, possibly because of her opposition to his schemes, and she continued to live in Wirksworth, where Richard had at one time set up a workshop for his barber-surgeon business prior to his patenting of the roller-spinning device.

Both Richard the younger and his half-sister Susannah married in 1780, Richard to Mary Simpson of Bonsall and Susannah to Charles Hurt of Wirksworth. Sir Richard, 'a difficult man to those who worked with him', objected to his son's marriage, even though Mary came from a family which had built a fortune from lead mining. Therefore Mary's father, Adam, had a background resembling that of Sir Richard.

Sir Richard died on 3rd August 1792, aged 59, at Rock House, which he had occupied since 1776, his first and only home in Cromford. Apart from making generous provision in his will for Margaret (who died on Christmas Day, 1811, still living in Wirksworth), his daughter Susannah, his sisters and various grandchildren, nephews and nieces, he left the greater part of his fortune, including his entire cotton-spinning empire to his son, Richard.

The younger Richard had done much to create his own fortune, having invested in the government stock market from the 1780s, adding to his father's already impressive holdings, and he eventually became the largest holder of government funds in England: by 1822 his holding of these funds had risen to more than £1 million. He bought shares in turnpike roads, canals and railways at a time when the transport section of the Industrial Revolution provided many investment opportunities. He made personal loans to several members of the aristocracy and gentry, including, in Derbyshire alone, Georgiana, Duchess of Devonshire, wife of the 5th Duke (subject of recent biographies by Amanda Foreman and Lyndsey Porter as well as a much-acclaimed film), Sir Thomas Hunloke, Bart., of Wingerworth Hall, the Earl of Chesterfield, Edward Miller-Mundy of Shipley and William Drury-Lowe of Locko Park as well as many local business men.

The younger Richard had good reasons for buying the Sutton Scarsdale estate: apart from his policy of providing homes for his sons which reflected the family's tremendous wealth, as a very astute businessman he was attracted by the profit potential from the minerals which lay under the estate. Samuel Oldknow, a business associate (and a former partner of Sir Richard), wrote to Richard from Mellor, Cheshire on 20th November 1824, approving the purchase of the estate:

'I do most sincerely rejoice that you have bought Sutton Hall estates. I received the News here last night from W. B. Thomas Esq. who adds – for *216,000£* which I have no difficulty in saying is *cheap* ... I am told the Estate abounds with *untaped* [sic] minerals.'

Oldknow, himself a major shareholder and leading figure in the building and operation of the Peak Forest and Cromford Canals, was acutely aware of the necessity of a good transport system so that minerals – chiefly coal and ironstone on the Sutton Scarsdale Estate – could be sold on the commercial market.

Richard died in April 1843, aged 87, after possibly suffering a stroke and completing his financial accounts until a fortnight before his death. His body was borne from Willersley Castle to Cromford Chapel by labourers belonging to the estate followed by many relatives and friends.

There was also an immense crowd of orderly and respectably dressed people. Although it was a Saturday market day in Cromford all shops were completely closed. His sixteen page will, a remarkable document, made his remaining five sons the main beneficiaries. They inherited the estates that had been bought for them and each received a legacy which varied between £40,000 and £120,000. In addition the residue of Richard's estate was equally divided among the sons, each of them receiving £263,745 17s. Many other members of Richard's extended family received varying amounts of money: daughters, nephews, nieces, grand-children (of which there were fifty-five), as well as servants, hospitals and various other bodies including Derbyshire Infirmary, Nottingham Hospital and Manchester Infirmary.

Richard's fortune had been built on the inheritance from his father, Sir Richard, together with his own astute, shrewd and successful business ventures into government stock, landed estates, mortgages and banking: his banking business, Richard Arkwright & Co. of Wirksworth, provided much of his wealth. Any assessment or comparison of his wealth with that of other successful entrepreneurs, heirs and heiresses is difficult, to say the least, but at his death he was almost certainly the richest commoner of the first half of the 19th century in England and possibly the richest commoner in Europe: William Gardiner wrote in 1838 that 'excepting Prince Esterhazy, he is the richest man in Europe'.

According to Tom and Peter Arkwright's research the total family fortune was over £5,000,000 of which Richard held approximately £3,720,000 (over £150,000,000 today). Richard and his father, therefore, had established a dynasty of descendants who continued to buy into landed property, taking over some of the greatest country estates in England. They were not members of the aristocracy but landowners, fundholders and significant members of the upper-middle class 'nouveau riche', although several members of the extended family married into the aristocracy and gentry as Arkwrights have continued to do to the present day.

2

The Hall and its Occupants before the Arkwrights

Sutton Scarsdale Hall and the estate associated with it have a fascinating history which has been well documented by local historian Pamela Kettle and which is summarised here. The land upon which the Hall stands was originally owned by Wulfric Spott, a Saxon officer attached to the court of King Ethelred. The name 'Sutton' derives from 'Sudtune', meaning south of a farm or settlement, in this case the settlement, according to Pamela Kettle, almost certainly being Staveley. At Spott's death in 1002 he left a large area of land to the monks of Burton Abbey: they owned it, along with other landed areas in Derbyshire until the Norman invasion of 1066, when William 1st took it and gave it to Roger de Poitou of Normandy, probably for services rendered at the successful conquest: he held 120 acres under plough; there was a mill and woodland providing pasture for pigs.

Partly because of the feudal system introduced by William, the land passed through various owners. In 1255 the land was given by Henry III to Peter de Hareston who rented it out and whose descendant, Lucia, married her cousin Sir Richard de Grey. A descendant, Alicia de Grey, married John Leake (variously also spelt Leek or Leeke) of Nottinghamshire in 1401, and so the land came into the ownership of the Leake (the final accepted spelling) family where it remained for 339 years until sold in 1740 to the Clarke family. It is to Nicholas Leake, the fourth Earl of Scarsdale, that we must look for the building of the Hall which Richard

Arkwright (son of Sir Richard) bought, the shell of which stands today.

It is likely that the first building on the site was a medieval hall facing north/south. The discovery of two medieval tiles verified by Beverley Nenk of the British Museum possibly dating to the late 14th century, as well as their close situation to the church of St Mary, seem to support this.

Several structural changes took place over the centuries since the original hall was built and Richard Sheppard in his 'Sutton Scarsdale Hall, Derbyshire' report for English Heritage has indicated that the earliest specific reference to a hall was in 1570 followed by 1595. The hall that Nicholas Leake commissioned was, according to the report either the fourth or, quite probably, the fifth building on the site. The hall which existed during the English Civil War when the owner was Sir Francis Leake, a staunch Royalist, who was knighted in 1604, created a baronet in 1611, Lord Deincourt of Sutton in 1624 and Earl of Scarsdale in 1645 was attacked and pillaged by Colonel Thomas Gell, brother of Sir John Gell of Hopton Hall. The Gells were the leading Parliamentarians in Derbyshire and had established a base at Bolsover Castle from where Thomas Gell attacked Sutton Scarsdale Hall with 500 men and two cannons. The hall was damaged and abandoned for several years after Sir Francis fled to Newark and was taken prisoner. Parliamentarians pillaged the hall and probably caused major damage. Sir Francis was allowed back to Sutton Scarsdale on condition that he paid £18,287 to buy the estate back, an amount his son procured from friends and relatives.

At some stage in the 17th century formal gardens were laid out around the Hall, the deer park being reduced in size and the avenues of trees planted. After the 2nd and 3rd Earls of Scarsdale, Nicholas and Robert, Nicholas Leake inherited 'a poor howse', and there are several possible reasons why he, as the 4th Earl of Scarsdale, decided to enlarge and rebuild Sutton Scarsdale Hall. Owners tended to use existing sites to cut down the cost of complete rebuilding, for nostalgic reasons, to leave a legacy of building or because of the ideal position their house occupied. Certainly Sutton Scarsdale Hall was situated in an enviable position; built at the summit of a gentle slope, views across the ha-ha from the eastern and northern fronts encompassing the deer park, avenues of trees, lakes and parks and across the valley to the outline of Bolsover Castle situated on the scarp slope of the Vale of Scarsdale must have been breath-taking, as they are today. North-east Derbyshire initially contained a high density of country houses and today, of the remaining 62 country houses within a 15km (10 mile) radius of Sutton Scarsdale Hall, half were rebuilt or drastically altered in the 18th century, as was Sutton Scarsdale Hall itself.

At this time there was also a strong link between Tories: since the accession to the throne of William of Orange in 1688, Tories were suspected of supporting the Catholic, Jacobite cause: many Tories (out of favour politically) returned to their estates. The 1701 Act of Settlement, which showed that parliament had a direct influence in the monarchical succession, had stated that the successor to Queen Anne was to be Protestant despite 57 members of the Stuart family having a more legitimate claim to the throne. The nearest Protestant contender for the English throne was the Dowager Duchess of Hanover: she died in 1712, leaving her son George as her successor; he became George 1st on the death of Queen Anne in 1714, beginning the Georgian period which lasted until the accession of Queen Victoria in 1837. There was a preoccupation within the gentry and aristocratic classes with increasingly spacious and comfortable houses, both for family convenience and for status and there was often competition with the owners of other large estates. Francis Smith, the architect of Sutton Scarsdale Hall, James Gibbs, Smith's long-term associate and Nicholas Leake were all Tories.

According to Professor Andor Gomme's detailed biography *Francis Smith of Warwick*, Smith, having trained as a master-mason, had become well established as an architect, working intensively in Derbyshire: whilst the Corinthian style Sutton Scarsdale Hall was being constructed between 1724 and 1728 from Top Hard Rock from the Wrang Quarry on the estate, Smith supervised the building of Wingerworth Hall, 1726-29, and Alfreton Hall, remodelled Melbourne Hall and modified Calke Abbey, among other commissions that he had undertaken. As a master-mason and architect, Smith had built his reputation as a designer and builder of country houses for the Midland gentry, which led to his becoming famous and wealthy. He was honest and reliable and consequently acquired a remarkable number and range of clients who were almost all connected by family relationships. They were predominantly Tories of the Midland counties, connected to the aristocracy into which they sometimes married and they provided Smith with a clientele of customers larger than that of any other master-builder and providing him with more work ever covered until the emergence of 19th-century building companies.

Smith had, through experience, become skilled as an accomplished architect as well as a quantity surveyor. He had close building connections with a group of highly talented master-craftsmen and he knew the rates they would charge, so he could guarantee both the cost and quality of their work. In 1725, travelling only by horseback or carriage, he was engaged in building sixteen houses in six counties. In 1730 he had twelve major works to supervise; in 1735 the number was thirteen in eleven counties, his known activities ranging widely across the country as far as Lincolnshire, Wiltshire, Shropshire, Surrey, Cheshire, Gloucestershire and the eastern counties of Wales.

Throughout his career Smith was willing to accept commissions of any kind such as farmhouses, schools, modifications and extensions to existing buildings, complete houses and churches and, occasionally, consultancy work. He had a long-term friendship with James Gibbs, a member of the gentry class who had trained as an architect, completing his architectural training in Rome. Gibbs' building of Ditchley Park in Oxfordshire for the Earl of Lichfield, which had design similarities with Sutton Scarsdale Hall, may well have influenced Smith's design of Sutton and there is no doubt that Gibbs' influence is obvious at Sutton Scarsdale, but because of Smith's close association with Gibbs he would have known of many design examples that may have had something to do with the design of Sutton Scarsdale; Gibbs made no claim on it, and Professor Gomme gives Smith sole credit for possessing the overall vision and skilful ability to remodel the earlier house at Sutton Scarsdale. It may be that the south front of Chatsworth House, very similar to the east front of Sutton Scarsdale Hall, could have been an influence; Smith may have studied it on his journeys through Derbyshire. Any assistance given by Gibbs would probably have been in the early stages of design, yet it is

Smith who was totally involved with the project from its conception to completion. Gibbs repeatedly called on Smith over a period of almost 20 years, culminating in the design of the Radcliffe Camera in Oxford.

According to Professor Gomme, on the Sutton Scarsdale site, as on all other building sites, Smith assembled a team of essential master-craftsmen, comprising a mason and possibly a bricklayer, carpenter, joiner, plumber and glazier, possibly a slater or tiler, and later joined by a painter, plasterer and perhaps a carver. Some members of the team were independent and highly talented master-craftsmen who stayed with Smith in a kind of loose guild, following him to work on several projects. Smith also employed local craftsmen and was the controlling hand in the design of rooms, although he allowed individual designs of decoration, integrating the work of individual craftsmen with different skills and using different materials.

Smith's general way of working – and this was true of Sutton Scarsdale Hall – was to use his own direct employees to build the shell of the house, then a different team would join Smith to finish the building.

The names of those who worked with Smith at Sutton Scarsdale were recorded on a lead plate which would originally have been attached to the outside of the Hall upon its completion. The plate, kept safely in a private house near Chesterfield, reads as follows:

'This house was begun to be re-built in the year 1724, by order of the Right Honarable (sic) Nicholas, Earl of Scarsdale. Francis Smith of Warwick, Gentleman Architect. Edward Poynton of Nottingham Gentleman Joiner. Francis Butcher of Duckmanton Carpenter. Albert Artari Gentleman and Francis Vossali Gentleman Italians who did the Stukework (sic). Joshua Reading of Derby Gentleman painter. Joshua Needham Gentleman plasterer. William Jeffrey of Chesterfield plumer(sic). Thomas How of Westminster Gentleman upholsterer John Wilks of Birmingham Gentleman locksmith, John Lillyman Gentleman Steward. John Christian Gentleman Gardener John Nott Gentleman Keeper. In the year 1728 the Great Pond in the Park was made.'

The Steward, Gardener and Keeper would have been the principal employees on the estate at that time. Of the names on the lead plate no mason or bricklayer is mentioned, presumably because they were Smith's own employees. Only Butcher and Jeffrey were local and neither of them worked elsewhere for Smith. Butcher is known to have done flooring and framing at Sutton Scarsdale and may have been called in for additional work, for Smith would almost certainly have brought a carpenter with him. The Swiss-Italians, Artari and Vossali only worked for Smith occasionally because figurative stucco-work such as that at Sutton Scarsdale was only called for infrequently. The other workmen appeared together so often that they constituted an association with Smith for the finishing and decoration of his houses: Smith repeatedly called on them so that, as a kind of loose guild, they rarely worked outside Smith's building empire.

Thomas Eborall, the principal master-joiner, was a very accomplished craftsman whose work was exceptionally good; Edward Poynton was remarkably gifted, almost the last carver in the Gibbons tradition and a true artist in wood and marble. So the 'team' who worked at Sutton Scarsdale created interiors in the Hall well above what was expected of them: their craftsmanship was exceptional. As a master-builder, Smith had hardly any rivals among his contemporaries; the work of his bricklayers and masons was of the highest order and the bricklaying was never bettered.

Sutton Scarsdale Hall, like other great houses such as Chatsworth House and Calke Abbey, was re-modelled around an existing house. Architects such as Smith had to very skilfully utilise as much of the existing fabric as far as possible: at Sutton Scarsdale windows, doors and fireplaces were blocked in where necessary and new ones knocked through existing walls. Sutton Scarsdale Hall was one of the most ambitious building projects attempted by Francis Smith and it was undeniably a 'Smith' house, yet he was restricted by what existed already. Each of the three or four houses that had existed on the site had been extended and rebuilt over the centuries and the existing architecture must have presented great difficulties. The arrangement of the rooms designed by Smith was very much conditioned by the re-use of much of the existing walling of the previous houses.

The completed Hall at Sutton Scarsdale contained the best baroque architecture and the interiors matched the exterior in quality. Smith constructed a grand Georgian mansion around the core of a sixteenth-century H-plan house, which had a hall running north-south, a projecting parlour range to the north and a kitchen to the south. Both wings had been extended westwards, perhaps about 1600.

Smith managed to provide a parade of seven principal rooms, with a further large drawing room/ballroom above the entrance hall. Smith's re-modelling had increased the floor space of the previous house by up to 45% and the number of rooms was almost doubled: the modified Hall had 45 hearths compared to 26 in the previous Hall. Indeed Smith was especially skilled in adapting an existing house to a client's requirements while simultaneously creating a new architectural expression. According to Professor Gomme, Sutton Scarsdale Hall was a fine example of Smith's ability to combine the two tasks and it was his crowning achievement as a country house designer.

Smith had constructed four symmetrical facades, each quite different from the others. The finest of these is the east front which faces Bolsover Castle across the valley and which is the front seen from the M1 motorway. According to Professor Gomme this front is Francis Smith's joint-best piece of individual architectural design, along with the front of Warwick Court House. At Sutton each front was different to the others. The south range is eleven bays long, and is so near to the church that it cannot be seen in one view; it has three storeys for the use of servants within the same height which, in the rest of the Hall, has only two. The west front, facing the drive to the north front entrance which went past it has a recessed central court yard which is faced in stucco rather than stone because it contained the servants' hall, butler's pantry and 17th century kitchen. The north and east fronts were each nine bays long.

As a well-respected craftsman, family man and public figure, Francis Smith had fathered six children, three of whom survived into adulthood. It was the practice that sons of the same family should each be trained in different branches of the trade. William, the eldest, born in 1705, became his father's right-hand man as well as a mason, taking over the business at his father's death in 1738. Another son, Francis, born in 1707, worked for his father but he unfortunately died when Sutton Scarsdale

Hall was being built. He is buried in the church at Sutton Scarsdale, the inscription on his tomb slab reading:

'FRANCIS Son of Mr FRANCIS SMITH of WARWICK Architect and ANNE his wife who dyed the 23rd of April Anno Domi 1726, Aet 19'

Francis was probably killed in an accident on the site, where he was presumably engaged in the building work, although there is no evidence of that as nothing else is known of him. The third son, Richard, born in 1714, became a carpenter.

Nicholas Leake died in 1736, aged 54. He had never married, but he, a well-known figure in London society and his mistress, Margaret Seymour of Holborn, a member of a wealthy family, had produced three children, Margaret, Seymour and Nicholas. At his death, the amount of Nicholas' debt, presented to the Court of Chancery in London, was stated to be £97,116.15s. 3 3/4 d. His children also failed the Certificate of Legitimacy, so the Hall and estate had to be sold; they were bought in 1740 by Godfrey Clarke of Somersall (Chesterfield) Chilcote (Staffordshire) and Ulcombe (Kent): he was the descendant of an immensely rich, prominent merchant. The interior of the Hall had to be finished by the Clarke family – presumably Nicholas Leake's massive debts had prevented completion; the Hall fittings were only completed slowly as work on the Hall's interior was still being carried out in the 1730s and the 'best' staircase made by Thomas Eborall was only installed in 1748.

According to Richard Sheppard's account of the history of the Hall, Godfrey Clarke and his son, Godfrey Bagnall Clarke, died in the same year 1774: the Sutton Scarsdale estate had enormous debts and the Hall remained unoccupied for some time. Clement Kinnersley, of Loxley Hall in Staffordshire, and a cousin of Godfrey Bagnall Clarke, was given permission to supervise the estate: he modified St. Mary's church, provided new buildings such as houses, dog kennels, a coach house and stables, had walls, cottages and farms repaired and re-built and increased facilities for servants in the area which is now used as a car park. He supervised alterations to the Hall, including having some statues removed from the Hall's balustrade. A steam engine was installed in 1803 to supply the Hall and premises with water.

Because his cousin Sarah's son died in 1802 at the age of 16,

Kinnersley spent an increasing amount of time at Sutton Scarsdale Hall until his own death in 1815 when the estate reverted to the Clarke family. On the 17th March 1805, Anne Maria Katherine, the only child of Job Hart Price Clarke and grand-daughter of Godfrey Bagnall Clarke had married Walter (Baron Butler) of Kilkenny Castle, Ireland; he became the 18th Marquis of Ormonde in 1815 and they lived only occasionally at Sutton Scarsdale Hall, spending much of their time in Ireland. On the 18th Marquis's death in August 1820, his brother James, the 19th Earl, petitioned parliament for permission to sell the estate in order to help pay off the 18th Earl's debts which amounted to £450,000. The sale of the total Clarke estate raised £482,432. 10s. When the younger Richard Arkwright bought the Hall and estate in 1824 they were neglected and he spent money on improvements prior to the estate's takeover by Robert.

The new Sutton Scarsdale Hall was probably designed to house a maximum of 30 people, including residential staff. The layout of the rooms reflected the social divisions at the time between family and visitors on the one hand and staff on the other. Smith's design had been so effectively complete that the use of rooms hardly changed between ownership of the Hall by Nicholas Leake, the Clarkes and the Arkwrights. Any alterations were minor ones, an example being the windows of the southern wall of the smoking room being blocked in, presumably to create a flat, windowless, internal wall, and outside, carved into one of the stones used to block one of the windows is 'John Marsh, 1771'. John Marsh could have been the mason employed to do the work, as the inscription is delicately carved, or as Richard Sheppard has suggested, Marsh, born in 1709 and dying in 1790 could have been a prominent member of the community.

The Hall was the focal point both of the physical estate which surrounded it and of the local economy which it supported. The earlier Halls had a formal garden, deer park, archery ground and croquet lawn, which were probably modified during the 18th century when the present Hall was built, to a mainly grassed area. The working estate of farms and cottages provided rental and business income for the Hall's owners. There is no doubt that Richard Arkwright the younger, a man of immense entrepreneurial skill, was attracted both by the acquisition of an estate which would represent his wealth and by the economic potential of the vast mineral and agricultural resources.

St. Mary's Church is only a few feet away from the south front of the Hall and the two are joined, initially by a roofed walk from the Hall into the north aisle of the church, and today there is a contrast between the church, a frequented centre of the village and the desolate grandeur of the ruined Hall. According to Harold Taylor's initial writing, modified by updates by the late Pamela Kettle in 1993, then by Janet Bradshaw in 2012, the first reference to a church at Sutton Scarsdale was in 1294 when the manor was owned by the Grey family who probably built the church. Some windows date to the 14th century and some of the wood carving is 15th century. Certain aspects of the church date from the 16th and 17th centuries and the roof has been raised twice in the church's history.

The church was modified in 1708 by new seating and in 1719 the West Gallery was installed: Francis Butcher, the estate carpenter, was responsible for both. A major refurbishment took place in 1807 while Clement Kinnersley was responsible for the maintenance of the Hall and church; the roof of the knave was raised, the windows on the north aisle were altered and parts of the tower and body of the church were renewed. During the 20th and 21st centuries the church has undergone necessary modifications and restoration.

The tomb of Robert Arkwright was discovered by Harold Taylor, a verger of St. Mary's Church and a Sutton-cum-Duckmanton parish councillor; he had to move the church organ because of woodworm and, upon moving the floorboards which were also rotten with woodworm, he discovered a vault which contained four lead-lined coffins; they contained the inscriptions of Robert Arkwright, his wife Frances and George and William, two of their sons.

1. Robert Arkwright

2. North front of the Hall (Nadin's Series)

3. Hall entrance drive and gates

4. East front of the Hall (Nadin's Series)

5. West front of the Hall (servant entrance) (Nadin's Series)

6. St. Mary's Church, Sutton Scarsdale

7. The gardens, Sutton Scarsdale Hall (Nadin's Series)

8. The gardens, Sutton Scarsdale Hall (Nadin's Series)

9. Lady, possibly a member of the Arkwright family, at the entrance to the Hall drive.

10. Gardeners at west front of Hall (Nadin's Series)

11. Frances Crawford Arkwright, née Kemble

12. Sutton Scarsdale Hall, drawing by J.P. Neale

13. Entrance hall (Country Life Picture Library)

14. 'Best' staircase (Country Life Picture Library)

Mr. Arkwright

requests the honor of

Mr & Mrs Sharp son & daughter's company

On Wednesday, July 17th, 1878,

In Celebration of his attaining his Majority.

Sutton Scarsdale.

Dinner on the Table at Three p.m.

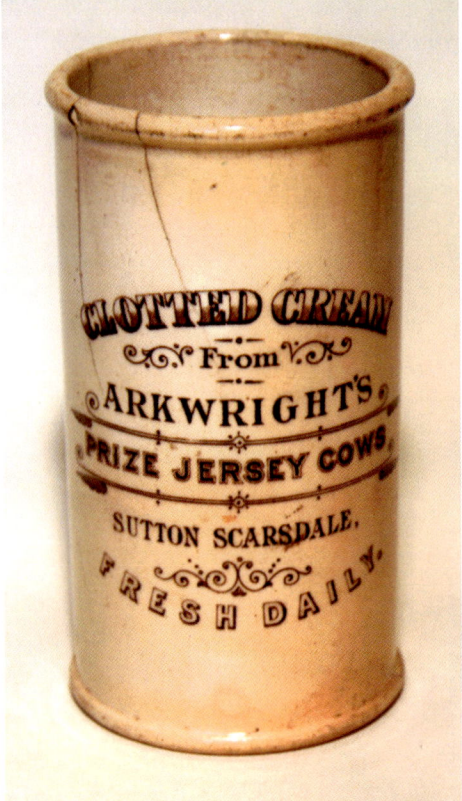

15. Invitation card to William Arkwright's 21st birthday celebrations

16. Arkwright's 'clotted cream container'

3

Robert and Frances: Marriage and Social Life

Robert, born on 7th March 1783, was the second son of Richard Arkwright the younger and his wife Mary (née Simpson). In 1796, as Richard moved his growing family into Willersley Castle, the eldest sons – Richard, aged 15, Robert, 13 and Peter, 12 – were sent to Eton. The family's connection with the school, still in existence today, had begun. Letters home, written mostly by Richard and recorded by Dr Fitton, contain references to food, boating, football, horses, flogging, fagging, holidays, tutors, masters, dames, and all the constituents of daily life at Eton at that time.

The letters also contain a fascinating glimpse of the Arkwright social life as friends and associates are often mentioned; for example, members of the Strutt, Hurt and Cavendish families who traced their strong links with the Arkwrights back to Sir Richard.

Robert probably left Eton in 1799, the same year as Richard, and in 1802 he was admitted to Trinity College, Cambridge, as a fellow-commoner. But because of the threat of invasion by the forces of revolutionary France, infantry corps had been raised at Derby, Wirksworth and Ashbourne, despite Derbyshire being land-locked, and therefore less threatened than many counties. In 1803 Robert and Peter both received commissions as captains in the Supplementary Militia; within four months Robert was in camp at Tynemouth.

Robert, at this time, probably first met Frances Crawford Kemble, daughter of Stephen George Kemble, actor-manager of the Theatre Royal, Newcastle-upon-Tyne. Frances was a cousin of the celebrated actress Fanny Kemble and niece of the legendary actress Sarah Siddons. The relationship between Robert and Frances developed quickly and possibly for that reason there was strong opposition within the Arkwright family to the news of a possible impending marriage. Robert's brother, Richard, was despatched to Newcastle to try and prevent a wedding taking place. He arrived too late; Robert and Francis had married on 27th June 1805, at St Andrew's Church, Newcastle, and had vanished. Richard, upon meeting Stephen Kemble to find out where Robert had gone, was informed that he and Frances were believed to be in Scarborough. Richard had already inspected the marriage register and believed the marriage to be illegal because of its recording in pencil, in an infirm hand, by an 84-year-old clergyman. He criticised Kemble for allowing the marriage to take place and wrote in a letter, dated Monday, 1st July, 1805, to his father, that he had 'called at the Kembles after their dinner, saw Mrs K. and two of her sons & from their very vulgar appearance and manners am quite at a loss to conceive how Robert could spend so much of his time in that company – I said as little to Kemble as I could, as he seemed to be a composition of deep cunning & artifice & in short everything that was bad...'

Following Richard's letter, Robert's marriage understandably caused great consternation within the Arkwright family and one can imagine the critical discussions that took place between members of the extended family as news of the marriage spread. Yet Robert had clearly seen qualities in Frances that were not evident in other members of the Kemble family. His judgement – which the memoirs and letters of his associates such as Greville, Harriet-Countess Granville and Thomas Moore all confirm – was in this instance superior to that of his brother Richard. Upon his marriage Robert was given £500 by his father, possibly indicating that there were feelings of forgiveness; in 1812 Robert received £3,000 from his father to buy furniture. In 1809 Robert had become a major in the Chatsworth Regiment of Local Militia.

Robert and Frances moved to Lumford Park, Bakewell, where Robert helped to run the Bakewell Mill with his brother, Peter, as his co-partner.

The Mill had been built in 1778 on the River Wye at Lumford on land leased by Sir Richard from Philip Gell of Hopton Hall. There were problems with the Duke of Rutland, lord of the manor of Bakewell, who complained that his manorial corn mill on the Wye was adversely affected, as was his fishing, by the new mill. Ownership of the mill passed to the younger Richard in 1783 then eventually to Robert in 1821; he left it to his son, the Revd. Godfrey Harry, who in 1860 sold it to the 7th Duke of Devonshire for £14,500.

At Lumford Park, Robert and Frances' first child, Charles, was born in August 1806 and baptised on 19th August, but sadly died in February 1808, and he was buried on 20th February 1808 at Bakewell Parish Church, where he had been baptised. On 20th August 1807, George was born, also at Lumford Park and baptised, too, at Bakewell parish church. About 1808 the family moved to Stoke Hall, near Calver, which had been rented by Robert's father from the Revd. Simpson. On 8th September 1809, William was born at Stoke Hall, followed on 10th October 1814, by Godfrey Harry. Eustace, the youngest son, was born on 27th December 1818 and the youngest child and only daughter, Frances Elizabeth, was born on 10th October 1820, also at Stoke Hall: she died in 1894 at North Berwick, Scotland, but was buried at Sutton Scarsdale. In 1817 Robert became a captain in The North Derbyshire Troup of Yeomanry Cavalry, then a Deputy Lieutenant in 1823.

For a short time at Lumford Park, then at Stoke Hall and finally at Sutton Scarsdale, Frances became a popular and engaging centre of Arkwright social life, exhibiting a simple, genuine, earnestness of manner. Her cousin, Frances Ann Kemble wrote that:

'In the society of the high-born and gay and gifted with whom she now mixed, and among whom her singular gifts made her remarkable, the enthusiasm she excited never impaired the transparent and childlike simplicity of her nature. There was something very peculiar about the single-mindeness ... in the middle of a globe of ice.'

Frances exhibited, as a member of nouveau-riche, gentry society, a simple-hearted genuineness which endeared her to all she met. Her aunt, Sarah Siddons, a confidante of Annabella, Lord Byron's wife was eventually a good friend of Richard the younger and his wife and they accepted her invitations to visit whenever they were in London : she was also a frequent visitor to Stoke Hall. Sarah Siddons was clearly a London resident of influence because of her fame; the original position of Cornwall Terrace in Regent's Park was changed after she complained that the new development would ruin the view from her home in Upper Bakewell Street. There is no doubt that Robert and Frances initially led busy lives, both socially and professionally. Sutton Scarsdale Hall and the estate had been managed by Robert's older brother, Richard, after their father's purchase. After Richard's death in 1832 their father took over management until Robert and Frances moved to the Hall, probably in early 1837.

Robert and Frances' move into Sutton Scarsdale Hall saw national improvements on the estate such as the introduction of land-drainage schemes, which improved many estates situated on coal measures, as well as the cultivation of specialist crops, the use of fertilisers, the appliance of scientific methods and the introduction of an impressive array of machinery for agricultural purposes. Robert, as an agricultural innovator, was elected President of the North Derbyshire Agricultural Society in 1837 and became a governor for the Royal Agricultural Society of England in 1843.

The Sutton Scarsdale estate was very large, comprising an area of over 5,000 acres, which included the area of Temple Normanton where the majority of the land was owned by Robert Arkwright. According to Peter and Janet Wright's 'Temple Normanton: A Thousand Years of History' in 1849 he owned 364 acres, while Mrs Packman (previously Miss Anne Lord, who married in 1847) owned 136 acres. The combined area was split up into separate parcels of land which were let to farmers and other tenants.

Very much an agricultural community, Temple Normanton had longstanding farming families: Richard Revill, born in Duckmanton, farmed 151 acres at Hall Farm; John Wharton, 90 acres at Manor Farm; John Wilbourne, 148 acres at School Farm and Joseph Cocking farmed 25 acres. Joseph Rolley lived in the Lodge house and rented two pieces of land from Robert Arkwright, for whom he worked as farm bailiff.

Robert and Frances were members of a wide social circle which included the Sitwells of Renishaw Hall; Georgiana Sitwell, daughter of the 1st Sir George Sitwell, wrote in her diary that 'Mrs Arkwright of Sutton frequently visited the Sitwells'. They were also great friends of the Duke of Rutland and, particularly, William Spencer Cavendish, the 6th Duke of Devonshire ('the Bachelor Duke'), known as 'Hart' to his intimates. He became, and remained, an admiring, constant, affectionate and devoted friend of Frances.

The 6th Duke, the son of the 5th Duke and Lady Georgiana Spencer, the fascinating and dissolute Duchess, led a very active social life, having several relationships with the daughters of aristocrats; according to James Lees-Milne he gave dinners and balls, house parties and shooting parties at Devonshire House, Chatsworth House, Hardwick Hall and Bolton Abbey. He stayed with friends in great country houses and appeared to be welcome everywhere. He was also a correspondent of Charles Dickens who, in June 1851, wrote to the Duke that 'I am in a favourite house of mine perched by itself on the top of a cliff': he was in a holiday home in Broadstairs that he rented every summer for more than two decades. The Duke had attended Harrow School with Lord Byron who was a close friend of the Revd. Francis Hodgson, who was invited to Newstead Abbey. Hodgson was appointed Arch Deacon of Derby in 1836 by Lord Melbourne; he also became vicar of Edensor in February 1838.

The Duke first mentioned the Arkwrights in a letter in 1812, indicating that he was to dine with Mr and Mrs Robert Arkwright in order to meet Sarah Siddons. The Duke must have known the Arkwrights before this date but it is not known when they first became acquainted. The Duke's mother was in debt to Robert's father although the financial dealings between them had been kept secret. According to Lindsey Porter, at Georgiana's death Richard Arkwright informed the 5th Duke of her debt to him, an amount of £4,239; the Duke paid the debt.

Frances and the 6th Duke were certainly kindred spirits: the Arkwrights were invited to stay at Chatsworth where Frances would entertain with her singing often accompanied on piano by Charles Coote, a permanent member of the Duke's household earning £200 per year and a dedicated and talented musician and composer. In 1832, the 13-year-old Princess Victoria, accompanied by her mother the Duchess of Kent and her German governess came to stay at Chatsworth and on Sunday evening, 21st October, was entertained by Frances Arkwright who sang, as the Princess later wrote, 'quite beautifully and with so much expression'. Sir George Sitwell and his wife also attended the occasion. Strong links between the Arkwrights and the Sitwells were evident when Robert Arkwright attended the wedding of Susan Alice Sitwell (eldest daughter of Sir George Sitwell) to the Hon. Wellington Stapleton Cotton in 1844. Music was Frances' passion and she was well known for her sweet, melodious voice; she sang hymns as well as popular ballads and poems by, for example, Tom Moore, Byron and Shelley, all set to music by herself.

Some contemporaries of Frances and the 6th Duke assumed that they were lovers because the Duke was well-travelled, lived a life of luxury and had several affairs with mistresses, but it is much more likely that this relationship was platonic. Frances was always invited to Chatsworth with Robert and the Duke always visited Sutton Scarsdale openly, even though he and Frances spent hours talking together, sometimes crying together, while Robert busied himself with estate matters. There are strong indications that Robert, like his father, was psychologically tied to his estate, guiding overall progress and wanting to oversee things personally. There is no doubt that there was a bond between Frances and the Duke formed of similar interests such as the arts and national events and gossip; the Duke confided in Frances with talk about his friendships and liaisons.

The Arkwrights were at times invited to meet the Duke's sisters and fashionable members of his London circle and the Duke also wrote to Frances when abroad. On one occasion, on the Duke's birthday, Sir Joseph Paxton fetched Frances from Sutton Scarsdale to Chatsworth to cheer up the Duke because he was suffering emotional and financial problems and Frances was a constant and reliable source of support. Through his friendship with Frances and his knowledge of the Kemble family the Duke, an avid and constant collector of books, pictures, furnitures and sculptures, bought for £2000 her uncle John Philip Kemble's (brother of Sarah Siddons) library of old plays in print and manuscript containing 7500 plays in 700 volumes; the collection included one of only two first editions of *Hamlet* to survive as well as the first four Shakespeare folios and 39 Shakespeare quartos. It was estimated to be the richest collection of its sort in the world. Sadly, the collection is said to have been sold in 1912 to contribute to the death duties which had to be paid after the death of the 8th Duke of Devonshire in 1908.

The only rift in their relationship appears to have been over political issues. In September 1841, a break in the friendship came about because the Arkwrights, who were committed Tories, opposed the Duke's equally strong support of the Whig party. The reason for the dispute is not clear but Frances may have withheld her true political views from the Duke and he may have felt betrayed, possibly believing that Frances had acted falsely towards him and had somehow let him down.

He was particularly vexed when visiting Sutton Scarsdale at election time and found it hard to contain his feelings. In addition, the Arkwright's son, George, was standing as a prospective Tory MP for the constituency of Leominster, in Herefordshire. Eventually, though, the Duke and the Arkwrights were re-united, albeit gradually. The Arkwrights appeared unexpectedly at Chatsworth while the Duke was showing his sister, Georgiana and some of her children around and the Duke was delighted. Later he visited Sutton Scarsdale to return the compliment and they had a long discussion.

After all it had always been Frances who supported and comforted him in times of distress and loneliness and the Duke continued to visit the Arkwrights often at Sutton Scarsdale. The Duke was also friendly with the Sitwells of Renishaw Hall. On one occasion, possibly during 1841, he visited Robert Arkwright on a Wednesday, then passed through Chesterfield on the same day on his way to Renishaw Hall, the seat of Sir George Sitwell Bt., where he remained until the Friday before returning to Chatsworth. As a child Frances was occasionally taken by her parents to Cullercoats, a small fishing village near Tynemouth, Northumberland. She had always loved the place and in her later years persuaded Robert to buy Cliff House for her. The Duke visited, became captivated by the village and bought himself a house there.

It is possible to build up an impression of Frances' character from evidence that is available in a travel journal that she wrote while undertaking a 'Grand Tour' of Europe in 1844: mention of her husband Robert also gives clues to his character. The journey through Europe took Frances and her fellow-travellers to Boulogne, Nice, Genoa, Florence, Bologna, Padua, Venice, Bene, Basle, Cologne, Liege, then back to Boulogne for the return crossing. Throughout the journal Frances made references to her travelling companions – Fanny, Frances and Robert's daughter born in 1820, John Strutt and 'Miss Strutt' (brother and sister – presumably John's younger sister, Elizabeth) The Arkwright and Strutt families had been linked by strong friendships and marriages since Jedediah Strutt of Belper and Sir Richard Arkwright had been business partners. They were also accompanied throughout their journey by a courier.

The tour started badly for Frances preparing for the journey

'...the last thing I did in London was very nearly to break my back: my maid inadvertently drew away a chair I had been sitting on, and down I came with a most violent blow on the back of my head, hurting my back also – anyone as heavy as I, would probably have been killed, but I escaped with very little injury and was able to reach Folkestone on the 16th of April with but little suffering – slept at the splendid new hotel there, and went on board at 9 o'clock.'

The journey to Boulogne was 'delicious'; the sea was 'a sheet of ripples... and the air was balm.' Frances sat upon the deck 'in a sort of dreamy delight', having 'scarcely suffered anything' from her back, and was sorry to reach Boulogne.

An interesting glimpse into the social life of Frances and her extended family is provided by references in the journal to, among others, Mr Greville, Lady Granville (one of the Duke of Devonshire's sisters) 'who ... most good naturedly came to see me, upon my return, at the Clarendon', Lord Holland, Mr Hodgson (provost at Eton), and the Misses Twiss, Thornhill and Barker.

Frances clearly missed home and relished any links with Derbyshire that she came across ... she met a boat engineer from Chapel le Frith (sic) who told her 'in a true Derbyshire accent that his mother lived, and that he had been at school when he was a little lad, at Stoney Middleton; he knew Stoke Hall well, and we talked about Chatsworth ... I am sorry to say he has married a French wife – and has no wish to return to Derbyshire. At ... We went next to see some beautiful tables in mosaic. These things I really think are done nearly as well in Derbyshire...'

On Wednesday 1st May, the group were driven in a postilion; Frances thought the driver looked like Eustace, her youngest son, and should have liked to kiss him.

At Pisa Frances was not impressed; 'As to the leaning tower I should like to have it layed (sic) to the ground – in my mind it is a very ugly thing and spoils the effect of the whole – even if it were upright I should think it ugly ... But as it is, it is quite an unsightly object, as bad as the spire of Chesterfield Church – which always offends me'.

Fanny was plagued throughout the journey by a bad cold and headaches: 'Fanny's cold is still very bad, and she is altogether very unwell; it is very unfortunate, for she was looking to being well, and I was rejoicing in the thought of taking her back to her father in much health and good looks'.

And again,

'Fanny has a little cold which makes me uneasy, but has borne the journey wonderfully, and I hope she will have a great deal of pleasure- I wish she had not preferred playing with a little black puppy to looking at Mont Blanc'.

On Friday 10th May in Nice, Miss Strutt too, 'was very unwell, she had caught a bad cold at Mentone, where she thought her sheets were damp ... So we remain here 'til Monday.'

On Saturday 8th June,

'My dear Fanny is far from well, the heat is too much for her, and has brought on a return of pain in her side, which destroys all my pleasure...'

At Nice the group were surrounded by:

'A large mob of children who yelled at us, begged of us, danced round us, gibbered their indescribable gibbing, made faces at us ... sang, halloed, screamed ... We were very glad to make our way back to the Inn as fast as possible ... for I began to be quite frightened ... the beggars are quite a nuisance throughout France, and Italy as far as I have seen of it'.

Despite the inconvenience and the recurrence of her painful back during a visit to the opera, there were many positive aspects to the journey. Frances and her group experienced some wonderful sights and interesting buildings. She saw the house the Duke of Devonshire lived in when he was at Nice and the house Lord Byron inhabited at Genoa; she thought the Mediterranean 'that most beautiful of all objects on this earth'; she looked at Raphael's painting of The Saviour, The Virgin and St John: 'I will tell the truth – I cried. I do not easily cry'.

On Saturday, 27th July, while the party was confined to Basle, initially because of Fanny's illness Frances wrote in reflective mood that:

' ...still we cannot get away but Fanny is better and will I think be able to go on Monday. For my own part our journey is drawing to near its end, I feel very curious for it to be over, and to get home: how I shall enjoy its quiet comforts; sitting for hours in my own arm chair, and no more packing and unpacking, no more sleeping in strange beds every night, no more bustling off at 5 o'clock in the morning. I shall have all the pleasures of my journey over and over again, and they have been great and many; and shall enjoy the absence of all the little discomforts, which compared to the pleasures, have been as nothing – the thing I am resolved upon, not to torment my friends in general, and my husband in particular, with my travels; but to content myself with one or two good victims that I know of, who will really like to hear all I can tell them...'

The party returned via Cologne staying at ' ...a very nasty inn' which 'put me in mind of Sheffield, Manchester, Newcastle and all the dirty English inns that are to be met with in our large towns.'

Arriving in Folkestone on Monday 5th August, after a very good passage, a final indignity awaited the party:

'...They were very troublesome at the Custom House at Folkestone in examining our things, they literally tossed and pulled out everything we had and I was very glad they had all their trouble for nothing; the only things they could have seized, which were some ... muslin curtains of the Strutts, and for which she was quite willing to pay, they never discovered – but they kept us so long, that we were not in time for the train and were obliged to stay all night at Folkestone.' The following day the party 'arrived in safety back again in dear, darling LONDON.'

Frances' feelings towards her husband Robert come through clearly in her writing. In reflective mood here she wrote that:

'It was very good of Mr A to let us come. I wish he had been here, for I am sure he must have enjoyed it but I fear he will never leave home – a bad habit – hurtful to mind and body. The mind is benefitted I am sure by such scenes as these'. She wished to show:

'the wonders of art to Mr Arkwright – how I wish he could see it – it is so impossible for me to make him comprehend it in the least degree...'.

Frances was clearly pleased to return from her tour after complaining throughout the journey of a lack of letters from home. On Tuesday 6th August she left Folkestone for Derbyshire, concluding in her journal that

'My journey has been delightful, what I have seen I shall remember with pleasure all my life – one of the most satisfying parts of my tour has been the conclusion at Derby, where the first thing I saw was Mr Arkwright waiting to welcome me home – the journey has been most agreeable from beginning to end, and we have been such harmonious travellers ... and I am sorry to finish my journal...(it has been a great pleasure to me, though sometimes I have been so pressed for time I have not known)... I am afraid it is very dull and that I have dwelt upon frivolities and omitted things of interest – if I ever go again, I think I shall do better – I have been bewildered with the novelty of everything, and too much excited to be rational – I am truly happy to get home again and delighted to see all the "dear familiar faces" I have been absent from so long – and one of the deepest feelings of my heart is thankfulness to God for having preserved us from all 'sad accidents and casualties' during our long journey'.

The journal gives a good insight into the character of Robert Arkwright: like his father at Willersley he was content to supervise his estate at Sutton Scarsdale in a most meticulous manner. He paid great attention to detail and Frances clearly thought that the tour would not have been of great interest to him.

The death in 1846 at Geneva of Eustace, Frances' youngest and favourite son, had affected her with irrecoverable sorrow and may have contributed to her own death on 10th March 1849, aged 62 years at Sutton Scarsdale; she was buried in the family mausoleum at St Mary's Church. After Eustace's death Frances had spent a great part of the last years of her life at Cullercoats where she had experienced a lot of her time as a child. Frances's death caused great sadness within the extended Arkwright family and their social circle. The Duke received the news, writing in his journal that he had been 'struck down – by news of Mrs Arkwright's death... Of all the strong attachments I have had in my life mine to her has been the purest the truest the most salutary. Oh how I loved her'. His love for her, of course was platonic but emotional: they had supported each other in times of stress or crisis and they had shared similar interests.

The Duke commissioned a lithograph of Frances Arkwright, based upon an early portrait by Sir James Hayter, which hung at Sutton Scarsdale Hall. One hundred and twenty copies were taken by Joseph Hogarth of Haymarket, London, at a cost of £40.5s.0d, which included the initial drawing on stone. The lithograph was sent to Frances' numerous friends and admirers, as well as to her own extended family. The portrait is almost childlike, showing Frances wearing a bonnet tied with large ribbons under her chin; her eyes are large and soulful, looking upwards. Underneath the drawing, the Duke, in his own hand, had written the emotive lines:

'So came thy ev'ry glance and tone,
When first on me they breathed and shone
New, as if brought from other spheres
That welcome – as if loved for years'.

Some 103 letters of thanks were inserted into an album and give a fascinating insight into 19th century gentry and aristocratic society. Local examples of the social circle who received lithographs from the Duke were Charles Currey of Heath, the Revd. John Hamilton Grey of Bolsover Castle, John Roberts of Chesterfield, the Revd. Humble of Sutton Rectory, Thomas Hallowes of Glapwell and Mr Palmer Morewood of Alfreton. Without exception recipients of the drawings thanked the Duke for his gift. The Duke's letter to Queen Victoria, written in August 1849, from London, reveals the affection he felt for Frances Arkwright:

'Madam,
Your Majesty spoke to me so kindly on more than one occasion about Mrs Arkwright that I cannot refrain from requesting your Majesty's

acceptance of a lithograph from a sketch that has been done since Mrs Arkwright's death – and is exceedingly like she was formally.

I have the honour to be,

Madam,

Yr. Majesty's most humble & most dedicated servant.

Devonshire'

Sarah Lyttleton (Lady in Waiting and Queen Victoria's representative) wrote back on behalf of Queen Victoria, thanking the Duke for his

'...account of the amiable and interesting character of Mrs Arkwright, and of reminding the Queen of the happy time spent at Chatsworth'.

The portrait seems idealistic, a view borne out by Frances' daughter, Fanny, who, writing to the Duke from Cullercoats, commented that

'There is a great resemblance about the eyes – the features that were the least changed – the rest of the face looks so much younger than I remember my mother that I am not able to judge of it, nor I think the expression is like that which had been in her happier days...'

This view was clearly also that of Henry Greville, who, writing from London to the Duke on 6th August 1849 expressed the view that

'It is to me a more pleasing portrait than if it had been taken in her latter days, when grief and suffering had cast their shadow over her countenance.'

One letter from John Strutt of Bridge Hill begins 'My sister and I...' and they are probably the Strutts who accompanied Frances Arkwright and her daughter Fanny upon their 1844 Grand Tour of Europe.

Robert Arkwright wrote to the Duke from Cullercoats on August 24, 1849:

'Upon my arrival at this place Fanny delivered to me the Print your Grace was so kind as to send to me and I now beg you to accept my sincere thanks for it.

I will take this opportunity of thanking you also for the very great kindness ... invariably shown to my family for forty years ... I believe that Mrs Arkwright was more sincerely attached to you than to any other person except <u>our</u> own family.

I hope that you are in good health, and that you have enjoyed yourself at Bolton'.

Clearly, the Duke had asked at some stage to be given some books, as mementos of Frances. His request elicited the following reply from Fanny at Sutton Scarsdale on 27th February 1850:

'My Lord,

I am afraid you will think I have been a long time in answering the note you left for me the other day when you were so good as to call here, and you will be no less inclined to excuse the delay, as I must not comply with your request – my father would be happy to give you any of the songs but he is reluctant to the idea of the books, which were her own private repository, being put now into other hands, he has sealed them up and put them away, and I think you will understand that makes them <u>sacred</u> still, if you can mention any.... that you would wish for, I shall be happy to copy them for you...'

A compromise was clearly reached following the Duke 's request, because in the Chatsworth archives at present are Frances Arkwright's 1844 travel journal, a volume of her words and songs (over 100 songs) and a journal of letters, replying to the Duke's gift of his lithograph, as well as many letters written by or relating to members of the Arkwright family, especially Robert and Frances of Sutton Scarsdale Hall.

Robert died on 6 August 1859, at Sutton Scarsdale aged 76 and, in keeping with his personal lifestyle, the funeral was conducted as privately as possible and without ostentation. The request of tenants to attend the funeral was granted; eight labourers employed on the estate carried the coffin which was deposited in the family mausoleum in St Mary's Church after the service, which was conducted by the Revd. M.M. Humble. Chief mourners were the Revd. Godfrey Harry Arkwright (successor to the estate), Peter Arkwright, Sir Hew Dalrymple and Francis Hurt. In his complex seven-page will, dated 25 January 1858, he made considerable provision for members of his extended family and house servants. He also left the trustees to invest money in government, or railway or other bonds so that the income could go to members of his family. Robert entailed the Sutton Scarsdale Estate upon his only surviving son Godfrey as tenant for life, and then upon his grandson William.

4

Life at the Hall

In the earlier houses built on the current Sutton Scarsdale Hall site, servants may well have slept in the same rooms as their employers; until the 18th century this was common practice. Servants would be tucked up in a smaller bed that could be stored during daylight hours so as to be close at hand. They also 'waited' upon their superiors, standing in attendance and constantly within earshot if not actually in the same room. The advantage was in having a servant on call, day and night. It is very likely that servants were recruited locally from tenant farmers, estate workers and existing servants' families. According to Jeremy Musson, household servants from these groups had no aspirations to copy the status of their employers, as some well-born attendants had. By the 1730s the number of these attendants as a feature of aristocratic households had virtually disappeared.

There is no documentary evidence showing how Halls were run although it is likely that the present Sutton Scarsdale Hall servants were recruited in the same way when it was first built. Tenants' children had a well-developed sense of deference and an understanding of what service involved: they could be trained by their parents or siblings who were already working in the Hall. In this way successive generations of the Leake and Clarke families probably came to be served by the children and grandchildren of locally born servants and a mutual reliance would have been established between the families of Sutton Scarsdale Hall and the local retainers.

Gradually the physical proximity of master and servant began to change with the new notions of privacy. It was hard to keep personal secrets from other members of the household as discussions or quarrels, for example, were likely to be overheard. The creation of servants' quarters, when servants were summoned by a long-distance bell board, usually located in the servants' hall or in a corridor of the servants' wing, changed the relationship forever, according to Sian Evans, between employer and employee. Servants and their duties became invisible as discreet backstairs were provided for the exclusive use of staff. Servants, formerly spending their days observing a family, listening to conversations, enjoying the warmth, comfort, light and furnishings of some of the best rooms in the house, now had to stay in their own quarters until summoned by a ringing bell.

By the 18th century this arrangement had become the norm as families withdrew to their own private rooms. Although the Sutton Scarsdale Hall household, like any other house of its type, had a very strict hierarchy within which each servant knew their place, over a period of many years some members of staff may well have formed a bond with the family or some of the family members, but the line between the family and staff would never have been crossed.

The present Sutton Scarsdale Hall, within a park of about 280 acres of land, was built with exclusivity a matter of course. A suite of seven ground floor rooms on the east and north fronts, with bedrooms and a ballroom on the first floor were provided for the exclusive use of the householders, relatives and visitors, while the servants had their own quarters. So from 1728 when the present Hall was completed and householders lived separately from servants, the rooms were rigorously defined as 'front of house' and 'servants' quarters'. The service areas, including the servants' attic bedrooms as well as rooms for less important visitors faced the church in the three-storey south front of the Hall and were accessed by a narrow staircase. The service areas would include, for example, the kitchen, laundry, storage rooms, larders, scullery, bake-house, dairy, cold room, gun room and boot room. At Sutton Scarsdale Hall, several of these rooms existed in the area extending from the west front, which now contains the remains of walls and buildings and is used as the car park.

Kitchens in big houses relied upon various methods of cooking in order to prepare meals. The oldest houses still had a type of spit where whole carcasses could be impaled on a metal rod and turned. The meat would be cooked in the heat of the flames from the fire below, and the dripping would be caught in a flat tray underneath. In the remains of the kitchen at Sutton Scarsdale Hall there is a metal remnant in the chimney above the fireplace and this could be the remains of a spit. The kitchen was part of the house before Francis Smith's re-building and it was incorporated into the modified Hall. In the south-west corner, as Richard Sheppard has researched, the kitchen would be a self-contained unit within the Hall and at the centre of housing for the domestic staff.

Sutton Scarsdale Hall was designed to house up to 30 residents and visitors although because of its design and layout it can be assumed that the new Hall operated within a well-established pattern of use typical of Georgian England and fairly rigidly divided along functional and social lines. Few changes, in fact, were made to the Hall in nearly 200 years of use. The new Hall had 45 hearths, making it considerably larger than the previous Hall which had 26. A new suite of rooms was created on two levels and specifically for the use of the owner and his family as well as visitors of the same rank. A total of 33 bedrooms were available to residents, visitors and servants.

When Robert and Frances Arkwright left Stoke Hall to take over the running of Sutton Scarsdale Hall, farming was enjoying a 'Golden Age' and the Industrial Revolution had led to the growth of the 'nouveau riche', which included the descendants of Sir Richard Arkwright. Landowners had considerable mineral rights at their command and, like Richard Arkwright the younger, invested some of their considerable wealth in country estates. The parents and children (who would include an heir) would receive wealthy influential visitors such as the Duke of Rutland, 6th Duke of Devonshire, members of the aristocracy such as the Sitwell family and an assortment of relatives and friends who would come to stay, sometimes for lengthy periods. Some relatives, such as Elizabeth Thornewell, might actually live on site. The Arkwrights, like many other families of their social standing, if not travelling abroad or staying with other families of their type, spent time dining, shooting, picnicking, hunting and horse-riding for pleasure. Sutton Scarsdale Hall will have been run throughout its ownership by the Arkwright family and, like any other great house, by its staff. The Hall was built initially for the occupation of a landowning family as well as for a large body of servants to run it, whose duties included providing food, heat and lighting as well as the maintenance of precious contents and furnishings that needed constant care and attention. This was true when the Arkwrights were in residence.

Throughout the 19th century there was a vast expansion of domestic servants in professional and middle-class homes. Robert and Frances employed a large number of staff, reflecting the structure of the households of the gentry and aristocracy. Two distinct ranks of servants will have existed within the Sutton Scarsdale Hall traditional household. Using the 1871 census as an example, the 'Upper Ten' included the butler, housekeeper, cook, valet, lady's maid and nanny. The 'Lower Five', in contrast, formed the majority of the staff and included footmen, lady's maids (who assisted the family's young daughters), various other types of maid, coachman, groom, servants' hall boy and others. The servants' hall was the centre of servant life: at Sutton Scarsdale the servant hierarchy would exist so that certain privileges, such as the right to eat in the housekeeper's room, would be jealously guarded. Some staff waited on the 'upper', privileged servants, having no contact with the Arkwright family.

In the 1871 census of the parish of Sutton-cum-Duckmanton where the population of the parish was 700, the Arkwrights residing at the Hall were Fanny S. Arkwright (age 38, head of the family and widow of Major William), daughters Fanny (age 17), Emma (age 16), Sophia (age 15) and son William (age 13); Mrs Arkwright's unmarried sister, Elizabeth Thornewell (age 39), was also residing at the Hall. There were 16 servants apart from the governess – a butler, footman, under-footman, groom, cook and housekeeper, three lady's maids, head laundry maid, under laundry maid, head housemaid, kitchen maid, two under housemaids and a scullery maid as well as two servants in the stables. The Arkwright family would be at the centre of life at the Hall, following the pattern established in all great houses.

The birthplaces of the servants at Sutton Scarsdale Hall are varied and interesting. The 1871 census shows that, apart from Agnes Rouff, the German governess born in Wurtenburg, the English counties in which servants were born were variously Derbyshire, Herefordshire, Kent, Yorkshire, Lincolnshire, Sussex, Oxfordshire and Cheshire; one was born in London. These various birth origins suggest that character references had almost certainly been used to employ them. Although no other documentary evidence survives, it also suggests that various means had been used in the selection of particular individuals. According to Sian Evans, in many rural areas such as Sutton Scarsdale, it had been the custom to find servants at hiring fairs.

Advertisements were also in use by the 19th century; *The Times* and *The Morning Post* carried 'Post Wanted' notices placed by servants. Word of mouth was also common; some house owners asked friends and acquaintants, existing members of staff and local tradespeople to recommend reliable, experienced servants. Some individuals set up recruitment agencies for servants and this might explain why some Sutton Scarsdale Hall servants came from a good distance away. Sometimes senior staff with good reputations were poached; as it became more difficult to recruit good staff, discreet enquiries from a household member to a housekeeper or lady's maid often secured useful information about servants in neighbouring or rival houses, and contact could be made. Again, there is no evidence that this took place at Sutton Scarsdale Hall, but the widespread origins of the staff suggest strongly that some means of recruitment had been used.

During the 18th century re-building of Sutton Scarsdale Hall a stillroom was incorporated into the ground floor and the 1861 census records Ann Morton, a 23-year old servant as the stillroom maid. The stillroom was originally used for the making of oils, perfumes and herbal remedies and the mistress of the house would distil liquids. The stillroom maid would report to the housekeeper (Ann Salvador, age 43, in 1861) and be responsible for preserving and bottling fruit as well as providing non-alcoholic drinks such as lemonade or barley-water; the maid would also make buns, cakes and bread rolls, also possibly having responsibility for the best china, dinner services and tea and coffee services. Jams and pickles were made using the produce of the estate; fruit such as cherries and strawberries would be bottled or dried and all sorts of garden produce – cabbage, onions, gherkins, for example – were pickled. According to Jeremy Musson the stillroom maid would also lay out breakfast for the upper staff in the housekeeper's room, prepare trays for early morning tea in the bedrooms as well as afternoon tea in the drawing room, all this relieving the pressure on the main kitchen. As the 19th century progressed housekeepers took over stillrooms to oversee the making of coffee, jams, preserves and pickles as well as the preparation of afternoon tea for the residents. This may have happened at Sutton Scarsdale Hall because in the 1871 census there is no record of a stillroom maid.

5

Major William Arkwright

William, the third son of Robert and Frances Arkwright, was born at Stoke Hall on 8th September 1809 and baptised at the Church of England Bakewell Parish Church on 15th September.

After Eton, William, like many of the Arkwright descendants of Sir Richard who became cavalry officers, entered the army on 24th July 1828 as a cornet in the (Inniskilling) Regiment of Dragoons. He was promoted to lieutenant on 25th June 1830, then on 11th May 1838 to captain, eventually becoming major on 9th June 1846, before retiring around 1850/51: he had been in the 6th Inniskilling Regiment for over 18 years.

William's retirement preceded his marriage in 1852 to Fanny Susan Thornewell. He was aged 42 and living at Skerne Hall, near Wanford in the East Riding of Yorkshire; Fanny was aged about 19 (her birth is recorded as 'about 1833'). Their brief marriage was prolific, four children being born between 1853 and 1857; they initially lived at Dinmore House in Herefordshire, near to the estate of his uncle, John Arkwright of Hampton Court. By 1854 William and Fanny and their growing family had moved to Hotham Hall. William had made out his will eight months after his marriage and before his first daughter was born.

The years 1856 and 1857 were years of sadness for the Sutton Scarsdale Arkwrights: George, unmarried, died on 5th February 1856, suddenly in London at his rooms at the Albany in Piccadilly. He had been ailing for some time although none of the family anticipated that he was so ill; the cause of death was said to be 'a sudden attack of spasm at the heart'. News of George's death reached Sutton Scarsdale on the 6th, which was Farmers' Rent Day. The usual practice after the collection of rents was that the clerk would dine and celebrate with the tenants but on this day there was 'a great dullness at the dinner – no health drank or songs sung owing to the news arriving about noon'. An accident occurred in London when the hearse going to pick up the body overturned – the hearse was 'a deal smashed', injuring two of the coachmen and two of the four horses, necessitating a replacement hearse as well as two horses.

Eventually, the body of George Arkwright was conveyed to Chesterfield and the Hall, under the supervision of Charles Laughton, the Sutton Scarsdale Hall butler, who had travelled to London. George was interred in the family vault in St Mary's Church at Sutton Scarsdale. Ten of the workmen acted as pallbearers, having been given a black suit each. The mourners included Mr Hewitt, the Mayor of Chesterfield, George's brothers Major William and the Revd Godfrey Harry as well as Sir Hew Dalrymple Bart., (husband of Frances Elizabeth, the only daughter of Robert and Frances Arkwright). Charles Laughton received all George's clothes and Major William, the sole executor, received all George's real and personal estate. According to Daniel Gladwin's diary George was said to have died immensely rich, chiefly in cash. George Arkwright had an amiable disposition, exhibited an honourable and consistent conduct in parliament and had won the respect and esteem of every person who had the pleasure of his acquaintance. He was the political successor to John H. Arkwright of Hampton Court and was first elected on 8 February 1842.

After a short illness William died on 13th May 1857, aged 47, in Yorkshire at Hotham Hall, which had probably been left to William by some family arrangement. He left Fanny, a widow and four children under four years of age. His will made suitable provision for his widow, children, his friend John Gilbert Crompton of Chesterfield and Bathsheba Smith, possibly a companion prior to his marriage and a lady acceptable to the Arkwright family. William's body was conveyed from Hotham Hall to Chesterfield Railway Station and from there by a hearse and four horses to St Mary's Church at Sutton Scarsdale, to be buried in the family mausoleum. As a sign of respect all shops on the route were closed and all blinds drawn. The service was conducted impressively by the Revd. Humble and the chief mourners were Robert Arkwright, the Revd Godfrey Harry Arkwright, Sir Henry Dalrymple, Bart. and E. Thornewell Esq. A large number of tenants and servants also attended. Fanny, widowed by William's death, lived for a further 53 years. She lived at Sutton Scarsdale until shortly after her son William's marriage, then went to live with her daughter, Fanny, in Bournemouth. She died on 22nd February 1911, aged 78 and was buried at St Mary's Church, Sutton Scarsdale.

6

Godfrey Harry Arkwright

Godfrey Harry was born on 10th October 1814, at Stoke Hall and baptised at Eyam church on 14th October. He attended Trinity College, Cambridge University, obtained a B.A. in 1837 and an M.A. in 1841. He was ordained in the Church of England and became curate at Mayfield, near Ashbourne, in 1847. In 1850 he was appointed Vicar of Heath and Vicar of Ault Hucknall, both parishes being sparsely populated and both being near Sutton Scarsdale, the right of presentation being held with Sutton Scarsdale Hall. It is likely that he became Vicar of Heath when he inherited the Sutton Scarsdale Estate upon his father's death. Godfrey married twice, firstly on 13th November 1844, to Frances Rafella FitzHerbert, daughter of Sir Henry FitzHerbert of Tissington Hall, an ancient family who trace their descent from Henry 3rd. They had two sons and one daughter. Frances died at Mayfield on 9th July 1849, aged 25. Their children were Francis, born on 17th March 1846, William Henry, born on 23rd January 1848 and Frances Alice, born on 27th June 1849, but who died aged 14 in 1864.

On 24th April 1862 Godfrey married Marion Hilaire Adelaide Pellew, daughter of the Very Revd. George Pellew, D.D. Dean of Norwich, who was himself the third son of the famous frigate commander Admiral Edward Pellew who was rapidly promoted through the peerage and was created Viscount Exmouth in 1816. Marion's maternal grandfather was the 1st Viscount Sidmouth. The children of Godfrey and Marion, all born at Sutton Scarsdale, were Marion Ursula, born on 25th January 1863, Godfrey Edward Pellew born 10th April 1864 and Walter George born

22nd July 1865. In adulthood they all married and had children. At least two of Godfrey's second family were distinguished in the field of music.

Robert Arkwright was pre-deceased by four of his sons – Charles, George, William and Eustace. As the only surviving son upon Robert's death in 1859, Godfrey inherited the Sutton Scarsdale Estate, his father having entailed the estate upon Godfrey and then upon his grandson William, who was also Godfrey's nephew. Robert had left a personal estate of £250,000 , of which some £70,000 went in legacies to his daughter and Godfrey's children and £20,000 to William as well as £20,000 to the Sutton Scarsdale Estate, which eventually went to William. This left £140,000 to be divided equally between Godfrey and William. As tenant for life, the Sutton Scarsdale Estate had no capital value for Godfrey, so his £70,000 plus the £5,000 from his grandfather Richard, would amount to no more than £80,000 and no significant land in his own right as an absolute owner. Yet on his death Godfrey had an estate in Warwickshire valued in excess of £30,000 plus a personal estate of £300,000.

Godfrey's wealth at his death is hard to explain because it appears that he had increased his inheritance in real terms in the short period of seven years between his father's death and his own by over 200%. In their research into the family of Robert Arkwright of Sutton Scarsdale and his descendants in the male line, Thomas and Peter Arkwright assumed that Godfrey could not have increased his fortune in any other way without some inheritance which has not so far been traced. Godfrey died on 17 December 1866, at Sutton Scarsdale and William, the only son of Major William, inherited the estate in 1878, age 21. After Godfrey's death Sutton Scarsdale was no longer available to his family and they moved to Adbury House in Berkshire. Godfrey's descendants are still very much in evidence today, various branches of the family living in Britain, New Zealand and Kenya.

7

William Arkwright (The Younger)

William Philip Arkwright was born on 21st April 1857, at Hotham Hall, Yorkshire, and was one month old when his father, Major William Arkwright, died aged 47. The Sutton Scarsdale Estate had passed to his uncle, the Revd. Godfrey Harry Arkwright, and upon Godfrey's death in 1866 William was nine years old. The estate was entrusted to the care and supervision of his mother who, along with John Gilbert Crompton, became William's guardians for twelve years until he came of age and took possession as tenant for life. The Crompton family lived at Duffield Hall, Derbyshire, and John Bell Crompton, the uncle of John Gilbert, was at Eton with Richard, Robert and Peter Arkwright, and the Crompton and Arkwright families had clearly remained in contact.

During the supervision of the estate by the guardians the tenants were socially involved; according to the 23rd May 1874 issue of the *Derbyshire Courier*, farmers were invited to take part in rook shooting. Nearly 400 rooks had been shot and were equally divided among the tenants of the estate: a dinner, organised by Mrs Arkwright, followed and the remainder of the evening was spent very agreeably. William and his three sisters, Fanny Elizabeth (b.1853), Emma (b.1854) and Sophia (b.1855) were educated by Agnes Rouff and this, together with the frequent presence of his maiden aunt, Elizabeth Thornewell (his mother's sister), made for a matriarchal society in which William grew up.

William was educated at Eton, following family tradition, then in May 1875, at the age of 18, he obtained a place at Christ Church College,

Oxford. He only spent a term there before tragedy struck. According to the *Derbyshire Times* of Saturday 16th December 1876, William was present on Thursday 14th December at the meeting of the Rufford Hounds at the Elm Tree Inn at Heath – shooting and hunting were great interests in his earlier life. William was riding a prize-winning hunter and at about 2 o'clock was following the hounds who were in full cry across Captain Gaitskell's farm at Longcourse. At the end of a long day, rather than wait whilst a number of gentlemen passed through a gate, he attempted to jump a fence. The tired horse, having galloped hard over several ploughed fields, rushed through the fence which divided the field from a by-road. William was unaware that the fence was a double one and he was thrown head first into the road. The horse fell with William and he was thrown with violence on to some stones on the hard, macadamed road. William lay totally unconscious in a pool of blood, having suffered severe injuries to the side of the head.

Three of the huntsmen, Mr Oldfield and other gentlemen, rode off quickly to enlist medical aid and Doctor Walker and Mr Stamford were soon in attendance. Telegrams were sent summoning Doctor Gisborne of Derby, who arrived later but was unable to render further assistance. William was carried to Captain Gaitskell's house at Longcourse farm which was close by and where he spent six weeks in recovery. William had suffered a depressed fracture of the skull and Doctor Walker, assisted by Doctor Stamford, removed two pieces of bone of considerable size. There was an immediate improvement and William became conscious, spoke and took a little water.

When sufficiently recovered William was returned to Sutton Scarsdale Hall and treated regularly for a year by a London surgeon, Mr Prescott Hewitt, who arrived on Friday, the day after the accident. William recovered from his initial critical condition although he was lame, without full use of one arm, and possibly rendered impotent for the rest of his life. He was also obliged to wear a metal skull cap for a year until the bone had grown over.

William's 'coming of age' should have taken place on 21st April 1878, but was celebrated the following July, possibly because his sister, Emma, had died in April 1877, aged 23, and the first anniversary of her death would have coincided with William's 21st birthday celebrations. William was also still recovering from his serious accident.

Preparations had gone well for William's 21st birthday and the eventual celebration was a grand affair lasting three days. On Wednesday, 17th July, the first day, 300 guests were entertained at the Hall in large marquee tents, with dinner provided and music supplied by the Chesterfield Prize Band. As well as members of the Arkwright family and their social circle the guests included the chief tenants of the estate and some of Chesterfield's leading tradesmen. After the speeches, dancing took place in the largest tent which was lit by Chinese lanterns. A magnificent display of fireworks provided by a London pyrotechnist ended the evening's entertainment and the company did not break up until after midnight.

The next day over 300 tenants and cottagers of the estate as well as their friends from Bolsover and other areas were provided with dinner in the large tent followed by more speeches, music and dancing: William again presided, supported by his mother and other guests who had attended the previous day. On the third day dinner and tea, games and presents such as sweets, oranges and cakes were provided for children of the estate and the surrounding district and distributed by Mrs Arkwright. During the last two days of celebrations the band of the Chesterfield Rifle Volunteers provided an excellent selection of music, including during the evenings.

William was a man of intelligence and learning and he possessed an artistic temperament which he ascribed to his paternal grandmother, Frances. He was involved fully in the running of the estate, exhibiting various interests, attributes of learning and entrepreneurship, and had his accident not forced him to give up his degree one wonders what he might have achieved at Oxford University. He was eventually an enthusiastic breeder of dogs, horses and cattle, an author and an expert in various fields; he shot and fished and had a great interest in gardening which took an increasing amount of time in his later years. Sutton Scarsdale Hall became a social centre for his family and friends; on 18th July 1881, Florence Sitwell wrote to her brother, Sir George Sitwell, 4th Bart:

'We have been spending a few days at Sutton, and enjoying ourselves immensely. The grounds are lovely and everything most beautifully kept up. We were a very jolly party together; some of the men were great fun and most of them nice. We danced 2 evenings in the ballroom upstairs- to the instrument that plays all the dance music required if the handle is turned. On Wednesday we went a party of 23 in a ... carriage to Derby for the Royal Agricultural Show. Mr Arkwright got a first and a second prize for a Jersey and an Alderney. Hester was there with her husband Lord Alexander Paget, he is rather good looking, with iron grey hair and beard... The heat was very great and the next day we had it 83 in the shade at Sutton'.

According to Peter and Janet Wright's account the Arkwrights had always acted as benefactors to the whole estate which included most of Temple Normanton village: in 1882 the chapel was demolished and a new church was built. William Arkwright laid the foundation stone in June 1882, and the church was finished and consecrated in February 1883. William Arkwright donated £750 towards the £1,050 cost of building and Mrs Packman contributed £200. In 1877 the church took responsibility for the provision of a new elementary church school which was partly financed by William Arkwright. It was built to cater for 41 pupils on the recommendation of a school inspector because a growing number of children needed to be accommodated.

In 1898 the school needed to cater for up to 80 children and an extension, again paid for by William Arkwright, was added. The village population had almost doubled between 1851 (107) and 1871 (209) and the number of children had increased from 19 to 53 in the same period. Mrs Agnes Arkwright made several visits each year throughout the 1880s and 1890s when she formally presented the items of needlework, which the girls had made, to the pupils. On these occasions afternoon tea was served and sometimes a half-day holiday was granted.

Although the Temple Normanton colliery was closed by 1893, from 1882 the Staveley Coal and Iron Company had arranged some 63 leases from the Arkwright estate to enable it to extract coal from up to 5000 acres of land on the Sutton-cum-Duckmanton area leading to many air shafts, wells, coal pits and quarries existing on the Sutton Scarsdale estate.

The Staveley Company then obtained a further lease which led to the development of a new colliery in Temple Normanton. The new coalfield was wholly the property of William Arkwright, although leased to the Staveley Coal and Iron Company.

In 1881 William was received into the Catholic church although his conversion appears to be independent of his marriage which took place three years later. Frances Crawford Kemble, his grandmother, came from a Catholic family, but there is no indication that this had an influence on William's decision. On Tuesday, 8th July 1884, William married Agnes Mary Somers-Cocks; she was the daughter of the Hon. J.T. Somers-Cocks and a niece of the 5th Baron Somers. She was the sister of the Duchess of Bedford. She and William were married in a Catholic ceremony at the newly built Brompton London Oratory, and the tenants of the Sutton Scarsdale Estate celebrated with a dinner, in marquees on the lawns of the Hall, and with dancing and fireworks.

The guest list for the wedding reflected the cream of English society at that time: numerous dukes, duchesses, lords and ladies, earls, countesses, knights and gentry attended and the bride and groom received over 200 presents which included diamond jewellery, clocks, various items of silver such as trays, candlesticks, knives and jugs as well as numerous miscellaneous items. After the wedding breakfast, held at Agnes' parents' house, the honeymoon was spent at Eastmoor Castle, home of Lady Henry Somerset.

Agnes was a prominent figure in London society, being a noted singer possessing a trained mezzo-soprano voice, a pianist and accomplished musician in general. She was also a very capable linguist and a devout Roman Catholic. In 1891 the census reveals that William and Agnes owned a house at 54, Rutland Gate in London, which they shared with Agnes' younger brother, Philip, a Foreign Office clerk. Seven servants were employed at that time. The 1901 census of Sutton Scarsdale Hall lists William Arkwright, aged 43, as head of the family and 'living on means', a normal designation for wealthy residents. Ten servants were employed at the Hall, their births being registered from Sutton Scarsdale and as far apart as Scotland and Switzerland. William was also a member of White's Club in London.

In 1910 William purchased Oldcotes and High House, both of which bordered on his estate, from the 3rd Earl Manvers, who reserved the minerals under the estate, which at the time were let to various local colliery companies. Evelyn Henry Pierrepoint, the brother of Sidney William Herbert Pierrepoint, the 3rd Earl Manvers, had married Sophia, William Arkwright's youngest sister, in 1880. Both farms were part of the Sutton Scarsdale Estate until the sale of 1919. Both Oldcotes and High House are today privately owned and neither is open to the public.

As a man of considerable energy and interest in sport, William was responsible for starting field trials for spaniels and the first trial of the Sporting Spaniel Club was held on the Sutton Scarsdale Estate in 1899. In 1901 he was Chairman of the International Gundog League which had – and still has – the aim of furthering the interests of working gun dogs. In 1902 the Kennel Club authorised the name 'English Springer'. William had become a member of the Kennel Club in 1876, three years after it was founded and in 1878 he was elected to its committee, then becoming a Kennel Club judge: for example, according to the 24th December 1906 issue of *The New York Tribune*, William had been invited to be a judge of 'pointers, retrievers and basset hounds' at Madison Square Garden.

William became increasingly concerned over the tendency to breed show dogs that won prizes rather than breeding dogs for their working attributes and in particular those of the pointer gun dog in which he had a deep interest. His first book, *The Pointer and his Predecessors*, published in 1902 is still relevant today to those interested in shooting culture and the attributes of the breed. It took William, a pointer fanatic, nine years to research and complete and he learned another European language in order to undertake some of the research which he conducted throughout Europe. It was accepted that William Arkwright's book was the most famous and authoritative book ever published on the pointer dog and William was acknowledged as having the best kennel in England at that time. The final break with the Kennel Club came in 1907 when he resigned, stating that:

'...evidently the type of show dog continues to deteriorate ... to award prizes and championships to untypical animals is to stultify myself and mislead the public.'

William was a collector of antiques and an expert on Oriental porcelain, was well-travelled and said to be fluent in French and German, a sportsman and a great horticulturalist. In his earlier life he spent much of his time shooting and hunting but he devoted many of his later years to horticulture. At Thorn, when he moved to Devon, he planted acres of hanging gardens and established a magnificent collection of flowering shrubs and trees from all parts of the globe. Year after year he added to the plan of developing a whole hillside. According to Tom and Peter Arkwright he disliked modern art, was very tolerant and had a great imagination. William was not interested in being involved in public life, although he remained interested in public affairs as well as being a strong critic of ineptitude and political chicanery. He did, however, become J.P. for Derbyshire and was High Sheriff of Derbyshire for 1890.

William experimented with ideas, converting from Protestantism to Catholicism then to Buddhism and finally Agnosticism. He wrote four novels after the publication of his treatise on pointer dogs: *Knowledge and Life* in 1913, *The Trend* (1914), *Utinam* (1917) and *His Own Soul* (1920). *Knowledge and Life* is a book of prose and verse; *The Trend* is a fine, human story and *His Own Life* is a challenge to present-day life, reflecting his personal spiritual quest and deepest convictions. Perhaps the most intriguing novel is *Utinam* (Latin for 'if only'– an expression of regret and discontent); it is rather a strange fantasy and satire on the desire to change from what one is to something perceived as a better option only to discover that the new form brings unforeseen disadvantages.

The story traces the adventures of a cypress tree who has been given the nickname 'utinam' by a neighbouring tree. The changes she makes, aided by Juno, the Queen of Heaven, Venus, Diana, an agent of the Devil and Pan, are from a tree to a peacock, a lady, an owl, a Suffragette, then back to a cypress tree. The book probably reflected some of William's own beliefs and he dedicated the book to his former wife, Agnes, whom he had divorced.

In 1919 *Country Life* staff visited Sutton Scarsdale Hall, taking 28 photographs of the property at that time, before its dereliction, as well as four photographs, taken much later, when the Hall had been in a ruinous state for some time. Eleven of the 1919 photographs were published in the article in the 15 February 1919 issue of *Country Life*. Following the article William Arkwright submitted a letter to the magazine which was then published in the 22 February 1919 issue. William's letter read as follows:

'In your last week's issue your account and illustration of this house appear to be both excellent and comprehensive; but I think it might be interesting to many to reproduce the picture of Mrs Siddons which is hanging in the dining-room and is probably unknown to many of your readers. This picture is 8 ft. in height by 5ft 6in ... It is by Harlowe, and represents the great actress as "Lady Macbeth" of the National Gallery. Mrs Siddons was Aunt to Mrs Robert Arkwright of Sutton Scarsdale'.

In 1891 the population of Sutton-cum-Duckmanton was 721 according to Kelly's *Directory of Derbyshire*; the area of the estate was 4,353 acres of land with 16 acres of water; the soil was very fertile, consisting of clay soil and subsoil. Two thirds of the land was pasture. In 1901 the population of Sutton-cum-Duckmanton was 1,158 and 1,475 in 1911.

William, discovering that South Wembury house in Devon was for sale, bought it and the Manor in 1920; it was situated above the estuary of the river Yealm, near Plymouth. The Manor was originally owned by the Crown then by Plympton Priory, then sold or conveyed to various families and individuals, including Sir John Hele, a wealthy lawyer who had prosecuted Sir Walter Raleigh on behalf of James 1. Hele built a magnificent mansion of 42 hearths, overlooking the river Yealm and the sea; it was probably built on the site of an older house because of Tudor cellars that remained. Possession of the manor passed through the Hele family, then to the Hungerfords by marriage, then to General George Monck. Following several other owners of South Wembury House William, aged 63, re-named it Thorn. William retained the mineral rights of the Sutton Scarsdale Estate.

William clearly saw the advantages of the site – a fine climate and an excellent aspect. Upon his move to Thorn in 1920 he established great plantations, removing and transferring as much of the Sutton Scarsdale garden as possible. William began extensive building work which included the addition of a large black cupola dome to the roof of the house (removed in 1925 by the next owner of the house), as well as a remodelling of the nine-acre gardens to such an extent that they were reputed to be the richest in Devonshire. He renewed and terraced the garden, planting acres of hanging gardens, transferring all his previous plants and installing the Trentham Vases, 8ft high urns bought when Trentham Hall was demolished in 1911, along with other ornaments removed from Sutton Scarsdale. His book *Utinam* was reflected in the planting of cypress trees in a controlled, naturalised setting, rather than in a formal layout.

The present garden of Thorn is little changed from that which William set out and many of his plants are now specimens and unique to the U.K. Successive owners of the property have respected and nurtured his design and the garden today is very much that which he laid out in 1920, apart from some storm damage.

Graham Titchmarsh, gardener at Thorn, has expressed the view, quoted in Robin Blythe-Lord's book 'that the great variety of plants which include trees and magnificent flowering shrubs which have been sourced from around the world, give an impression of what it might be like walking in the foothills of the Himalayas or the Blue Mountains of Australia'.

William died on 19 February 1925 aged 67, at Thorn. According to Robin Blythe-Lord he may have had some knowledge of his impending demise because in the month before he died he toured the estate and surrounding areas making a 'last visit' and bidding farewell to many of his friends and employees. Despite his divorce from Agnes she came to Thorn briefly to help with funeral arrangements, clear up the estate and prepare it for sale: she then returned to 28, Brompton Square, London, where she lived for the rest of her life; she died, aged 81, on 26 September 1940.

William's death took place on a Thursday afternoon and because his will stipulated that he should be cremated and his ashes scattered over the garden without any religious ceremony, he was cremated on the following Saturday and his ashes were scattered around his garden on the Sunday. On the Sunday and Monday all his staff were paid off except for two who remained as caretakers. Research by Tom and Peter Arkwright shows that after William's death an edition of *The Times* newspaper contained an appreciation of William Arkwright's life sent by Mr Eden Philpotts, a famous author and playwright who collaborated in plays with Jerome K. Jerome and Arnold Bennett. In Philpott's opinion William Arkwright was 'a man of quality' with a:

'great gift of imagination, a virtue so often denied to the wealthy. The passing of William Arkwright leaves the world poorer for a great personality and many friends to mourn their private loss. He touched life at points so numerous and with such accomplishments that it is hard to say, among his varied interests wherein he most excelled. He was an author, an expert on oriental porcelains, a traveller, a sportsman and a very great horticulturist'.

William's estate totalled £18,000 in cash plus the house and contents which he left to John Arkwright, a distant nephew from the Herefordshire branch of the family living at Hampton Court; Thorn was then put up for auction later in the same year when the estate was bought by the Hon. Mrs Ida Marie Sebag-Montefiore, widow of Captain Robert Sebag-Montefiore who had died from wounds in Egypt in 1915. After 1938 when Mrs Sebag-Montefiore sold the house and whole area, the estate was gradually broken up as the stables, a farm and farmland, coastguard cottages; a wood and walled vegetable garden were sold off to individual purchasers, partly for residential development. Since 1981 Thorn has been owned and lived in by the Gibson family; it is a private house and is not open to the public.

17. Bolsover Station

18. South front of the Hall, next to the church

19. Farmers/tenants, probably taken on rent collection day: date unknown

20. The Station Hotel, Arkwright Town

21. Market Place Station (L.D. & E.C. Railway)

22. Arkwright Town Station

23. Staff at Sutton Scarsdale Hall 1903

24. Staff at Sutton Scarsdale Hall. Date unknown, but possibly early 20th century.

25. Sutton Rock (Nadin's Series)

26. Charles Cockburn, a former resident of Sutton Rock

27. Church adjacent to east front of Hall

28. Hall stables

29. East front of Hall, painting by Daniel Halksworth

30. West front of the Hall, painting by John Piper

31. Terrace wall from rear gardens of Palterton Lane

32. Sutton Hall in its current state (east and north fronts)

33. Sutton Scarsdale Hall in its current state (east front)

8

Social and Economic Development on The Sutton Scarsdale Estate

From the beginning of his ownership of the Sutton Scarsdale Estate Robert adopted a caring and supportive attitude to his tenants. After his older brother Richard's death in 1832 he probably accepted responsibility for the running of the estate even before he and his family moved in to the Hall. For example, on rent day at the Hall on 3 February 1835, he returned to the tenants 20%, making a total of 35% reduction from the rental of the Sutton-cum-Duckmanton and Temple Normanton estates since Lady Day, 1832.

Robert Arkwright moved to Sutton Scarsdale possibly in early 1837, officially taking over the management of the estate. This was a period of 'High Farming' in England partly because of the passing of the Corn Laws in 1815. Robert was one of a number of agricultural innovators; he was elected president of the North Derbyshire Agricultural Society in 1837 and a governor of the Royal Agricultural Society of England in 1843. There was great interest in this period and in 1819 The Scarsdale and High Peak Agricultural Society was founded, The Bakewell Farmer's Club in 1848 and the Derbyshire Dairy Farmers' Association, among others. Robert was also a member of The Cromford and High Peak Railway committee, representing a proposed railway from the Cromford canal to the Peak Forest canal, first becoming involved while living at Stoke Hall: Robert bought 10 shares at a value of 1,000 pounds. His brother Peter was also a member.

Despite the repeal of the Corn Laws in 1846, when many predicted the ruin of British agriculture, the next 30 years were a 'Golden Age' of 'High Farming' in which prices were stable and profits good. There was a great interest in agricultural movements in this period and, until his death in 1859 Robert Arkwright would have overseen great prosperity on his estate. As Gladwyn Turbutt has indicated, there was a great variety of cattle kept in Derbyshire in the late 18th century as a result of the Agricultural Revolution sponsored by breeders such as Robert Bakewell, and the breeds of sheep also varied considerably.

Subsidised by the government, the introduction of threshing machines and deep ploughs as well as improvements in land drainage on many estates on the coal measures, such as Sutton Scarsdale, all represented technical progress which Robert, from his position and experience, enthusiastically embraced. Prices for dairy products rose and, because of the engineering achievements of the Industrial Revolution, Derbyshire benefitted from a quick rail service to London and the industrial towns of the Midlands as well as from the flourishing liquid milk trade.

According to the *Derby Mercury* of the 6th February 1850, Robert Arkwright was an excellent landlord; he often gave considerable assistance to his tenants, supporting them by helping to provide winter food for their cattle as well as constantly employing as many labourers as possible on improvements and similar works. In early February 1850, he informed his tenants that at the time of rent collection they should pay 15% less than the required amount. Also, for many years, Robert had given an ox annually at Christmas, to be divided amongst the poor of the parish, and to which the farmers added £5 for the purchase of bread. At Christmas 1851, Robert gave over 50 tons of coal to poor cottagers in the neighbourhood as well as a gift of excellent beef, varying between 5lbs and 10lbs per family according to their wants.

Robert had also supported the existence, in 1835, of two public houses. 'The Rose and Crown' situated just above the present 'Arkwright Arms' was kept by John Sales who died in 1854 aged 52 years; it had previously been kept by his mother Sarah Sales. It then ceased to be a public house and became a cottage, although the site is now unused ground. 'The White Swan' public house was managed by Joseph Bennett in 1835 then by Matthew Oates, who kept it from 1836 to 1857. In 1881 Mrs Arkwright, widow of Major William and mother of the young William, closed it because, as she said, 'it was nothing but a den for poachers'. When her son, William (known locally as Squire William Arkwright) inherited the Sutton Scarsdale estate he reopened it as the 'Arkwright Arms'. The original White Swan building was situated in front of the present 'Arkwright Arms'; it was an old stone building situated next to the road and was demolished in the 1920s. The present 'Arkwright Arms' was opened in 1929.

The Adelphi Iron Works

During the Arkwright ownership of the Sutton Scarsdale Estate between 1824 and 1919 there were many changes. The area of Derbyshire which included the estate contained – and still does – natural materials such as lead, ironstone, coal, wood and clay. Mining, including the use of these materials, can be traced back to Roman times, then through medieval times up to the 20th century, so the industrial history of the area is very involved. Several separate late 18th century maps of the whole estate show many coal shafts, air shafts, old coal pits and old quarries, and coal and iron were mined on or near the Sutton Scarsdale estate as well as on the Leake-owned Hasland Hall Estate.

When Richard Arkwright the younger bought the Sutton Scarsdale Estate in 1824 the Adelphi Iron Works, situated on the estate, was in existence and representative of the earlier industrial history of the Duckmanton area. The initial business was begun about 1760 by the Smith family, led by John Smith, master cutler in 1722, who owned the works. The Smiths had, for generations, been involved in the cutlery trade in Grenoside, Sheffield, the family increasing their fortune through marriage and business achievements. In the late 18th century the Smiths and their associates expanded their business out of Sheffield, acquiring The Griffin foundry at Brampton in 1775, to which the Cannon Mill, comprising blast furnaces and foundries, was added, producing iron castings for military use as well as Newcomen steam engines; the site eventually came into the possession of Robinson and Sons ltd. of

Chesterfield. On John Smith's death in 1784 the business passed to his sons, led by Ebenezer Smith who exhibited considerable industrial ability. By 1791 a new ironworks had been built to the north of the old Griffin Works and the firm had acquired several enterprises at Hollingwood, Staveley, Inkersall, Hady, Calow and Stonegravels in the Chesterfield area as well as The Griffin Iron Foundry in Manchester.

Because of the Napoleonic wars and the threat of invasion by revolutionary France the Adelphi Iron Works was built about 1799 on the Sutton Scarsdale Estate as a munition plant capable of producing 900 tons of pig iron per annum from the furnaces; jobs were created for the sons of local crofters and crofter families took in foundry, furnace men and miners from elsewhere. Cannon balls and shells were manufactured for the East India Company as well as the army and small consignments were sent to Russia.

Associated brickyards, claypits, two blast furnaces, a foundry and ovens also existed as well as a modified Newcomen engine and other steam engines; because of the almost inaccessible position of the Adelphi Works a short, half-mile canal, constructed about 1799, transported goods in small boats to the Inkersall road travelling in a general northerly direction, then to the Chesterfield Canal (which had opened in 1777) at Staveley and Norbriggs.

The Smiths had been the earliest ironmasters to smelt iron with coke and the family seemed to have been very prosperous until about 1815. The Smiths worked iron and coal seams which included the future site of the first Arkwright Town village and from 1799 to 1849 a small community of coal and iron workers lived on Duckmanton Moor, centred on the Adelphi Iron Works.

The Adelphi Iron Works was run from 1820 by Benjamin Smith who rented 118 acres of land around the site: the original intention was to launch a new business for Benjamin's eldest son, Josiah Timmis Smith. Benjamin was the grandson of John Smith, the founder of the Brampton Works, and he and his cousin Samuel Smith employed John Charlton of Calow as the mining adviser when the works specialised in the manufacture of heavy castings: Charlton was tenant of the nearby Lodge Farm, farming 34 acres until his death in 1833 and his descendants worked the farm until the 1870s. The Smith family also owned another ironworks in Calow, east of Calow Lane and about 2.5 miles from Chesterfield. The Smith family lived at Duckmanton Lodge which had been built by Benjamin Smith and which still exists, situated on the main road through Calow. The Adelphi site, as well as the smelting furnace and casting house had offices, a weigh-bridge, pattern-making shop, lime kiln, brickworks and iron and coal workings.

By 1830 the Smiths, one of the most successful firms in Derbyshire, were in financial difficulties: according to Godfrey Downes-Rose's 'Duckmanton Moor, the Land, Industries and People', the company had failed to make a successful move from reliance on munitions contracts into new markets and they began to run down their Chesterfield and Manchester foundries. The business suffered in the post-war depression, collapsing in the early 1830s. According to Philip Robinson's 'The Smiths of Chesterfield', Benjamin Smith, in 1840, gave evidence before a House of Commons select committee that 'the Adelphi Iron Works were losing a lot of their markets'. The ironworks' blast furnaces, after a boom in the iron industry following the railway mania of the early 1840s, were affected by a collapse of prosperity.

The Griffin foundry was sold in 1838. In 1845, after operating the Adelphi Iron Works with mixed fortunes for about 25 years since 1820, Benjamin Smith and his son Joseph sold the works after the concern was declared bankrupt; 'Benjamin was short of capital and the Works was running down'. In 1832 William Elsam, Benjamin Smith's brother-in-law, had bought the Adelphi property for £6,099 but this only brought temporary relief and the partners appeared to have had no other alternative than to close down.

After the sale in 1845 Benjamin (grandson of the founder of the company) and Josiah purchased the rundown Stanton Ironworks at Ilkeston, using borrowed capital, taking on new mineral leases from Earl Stanhope for ironstone, coal and fireclay and building new furnaces on site. By 1849 Benjamin Smith and Company were declared bankrupt at the Stanton Ironworks, the work being taken over at a later stage, in 1855, by Crompton and Company, a creditor. The Adelphi Iron Works struggled to survive and was still in use after the Smiths departed but several coal and ironstone leases were put up for auction, along with some equipment, resulting in several companies taking over the mining leases to mine the coal reserves. Robert Arkwright persevered with the ironworks for a while which closed down in 1848; he then turned the land back to its original use of agriculture and estate workshops. The old saw mill attached to the foundry, the weigh-house and works offices were converted for use as a farm house to accommodate Daniel Gladwin's family and the pattern-making shop became the estate's saw mill for making carts and equipment for the Sutton Scarsdale estate.

On the 20th August 1853, Daniel Gladwin, chief clerk at Stanton Iron Works, after paying wages and working there for seven years and about four months, returned to Robert Arkwright's service. He had initially left Arkwright's employment in April 1846, when he became clerk to Benjamin Smith at Stanton Iron Works; he returned to Arkwright's employment because of 'the disagreeableness of the manager James Holt' at the Stanton Iron Works who worked 'solely from theoretical experience, without knowing the practical part sufficiently'.

On 22nd September, Daniel and his family slept at Mr Bunting's home in Sutton Scarsdale, the furniture having left that day, then on 23rd September Daniel's furniture arrived at Duckmanton works and the family all slept in the house that evening. On 26th September, Daniel 'commenced clerking' at the office for Robert Arkwright. White's *History and Gazetteer of Derbyshire* shows a farmer, John Gladwin, living in Sutton Scarsdale; he was a brother of Daniel but he left his farm on 26th March 1856. According to his diary, on 27th November 1853 Daniel went to Sutton Scarsdale Church for the first time since 'being at Duckmanton'. J.G. Harrod and Co.'s *Postal and Commercial Directory of Derbyshire* for 1870 shows Daniel Gladwin still living at Duckmanton Works.

On 5th February 1854, on farmers' rent day, with Mr Mills, the estate agent who lived at The Lodge, Daniel collected £2,678.5.s.2.5d, his first rent audit since his return to Robert Arkwright's service. He finished receiving rents at the work office by 2.00pm when the money was taken to the bank by Mr Mills. Daniel dined with the tenant farmers along with Mr John Noton (Chairman) and Mr Alsop (Vice-Chairman). John Noton was farm steward to Robert Arkwright and occupant of Longcourse farmhouse. On 2nd August the farmers' rent audit was £2,196.16s.11.5d; on 7th February 1855, the rent audit was £2,808.2s.10d and the money was collected by 1.30pm when the cash was taken to the bank. Mr Mills dined with the tenantry at an agreeable meeting. The farmers' rent audit for 1st August was £2,628.18s.3d. According to Daniel Gladwin, despite his specific supervision of the rental collection, Robert Arkwright and Mr Mills visited the office 'virtually every day'. On 6th February 1856, the farmers' rent day saw £2,931.11s.6d collected by 2pm, but there was a great dullness at the dinner because of the news of George Arkwright's death.

The Arkwrights were therefore involved in the problem of finding a solution to the Adelphi ironworks issue: they were opposed by the Barrows, founders of the Staveley Company, who desired the lease of the mineral rights of the Sutton Scarsdale Estate. The Arkwrights proposed the construction of a railway from the Sutton Scarsdale Estate and over the Duke of Devonshire's estate to Staveley, but pressure from the Barrows ensured that the line was never constructed for the Arkwrights because the Barrows were concerned about the Arkwrights having way leave over land they were leasing from the Duke, and despite Robert Arkwright offering the Barrows use of the proposed railway for an annual rent the Barrows and the Duke rejected all proposals. Baulked by Barrow's opposition to a branch railway from Staveley the Arkwrights cancelled plans for further mining on Duckmanton Moor.

Cottages at the ironworks continued in use until they were demolished at the end of World War Two. Until then the buildings were used to house families, including that of Daniel Gladwin who kept an interesting and informative diary during his stay there. Some of the tenants of the ironworks were miners and their families who lived there until they could be re-housed in the new 'Arkwright Town village', built 1897–1900.

After that, according to Godfrey Downes-Rose, the remains of the works' farm buildings on the site of the Adelphi Ironworks were used as offices and as a depot for heavy open cast machines. According to A.N. Bridgewater's account *The Adelphi Ironworks*, at the sale of the Sutton Scarsdale estate in 1919 the old ironworks, now used as a farm and farmland, was named 'Works Farm', providing a link to the past.

The Lancashire, Derbyshire and East Coast Railway

The origin of William Arkwright's railway can be traced back to the Adelphi Iron Works: the Smiths who had built the Iron Works worked iron and coal seams on surrounding land which formed part of Duckmanton Moor. William Arkwright's idea of an independent railway running to the east and west coasts was inspired by the huge, rich, undeveloped coal seams which he wanted to exploit beneath the Sutton Scarsdale Estate as well as from collieries in north-east Derbyshire and in Nottinghamshire.

Despite plans being prepared to sink eastward – expanding collieries, as well as several smaller ones being built on his estate, he realised that a wider market for his coal, as well as that produced by the owners of estates in Nottinghamshire, many of whom were sympathetic to his plan, needed better outlets than those to the north and south provided by the Midland and Manchester, Sheffield and Lincolnshire railways. Rather than depend on the complicated system of existing railway lines owned by various companies, William Arkwright believed that the time was ripe for a new railway.

Coal and iron were expected to be the main transport materials, although local manufactures along the route such as machinery, wire, soap, leather and glass of Warrington, salt and chemicals of the Cheshire district, silk of Macclesfield, limestone and dairy produce of Derbyshire and Cheshire, iron and cutlery of Sheepbridge, Staveley and Sheffield, agricultural implements, machinery and agricultural produce of Lincolnshire and fish from the sea were all expected to contribute to the traffic of the railway.

William's ambition was to link the east coast, involving a new port at the seaside resort of Sutton-on-sea on the Lincolnshire coast with the west coast to Warrington on the Manchester Ship Canal and then by direct communication to the Irish Sea. It was anticipated that the import traffic of Liverpool and Sutton-on-sea would increase because of the additional trade with American and North European ports. There were also hopes of attracting tourists to Sherwood Forest and to the area of large estates known as 'The Dukeries': Edwinstowe was to be the centre of the east to west tourist traffic as a convenient centre for visiting these surrounding ducal estates.

Following an independent proposal, published in 1887, to build a Chesterfield and Lincoln Direct Railway, partly across the Sutton Scarsdale Estate, William Arkwright's scheme was released to the public in November 1890. The main national railway system, sponsored by the Industrial Revolution, had been laid by 1851 but many changes were taking place: new schemes such as Arkwright's were being put forward, although fraught with financial risk.

Continual opposition to Arkwright's intention to exploit reserves of coal and iron was provided by Richard Barrow, owner of The Staveley Ironworks. He had leased coal and iron seams around Staveley and Inkersall from their owner, the Duke of Devonshire, and saw any plan for a new railway as a threat to his own monopoly of the local coal and iron business.

The Lancashire, Derbyshire and East Coast railway (also known as the L.D and E.C Railway), with a proposed length of 170 miles, received Royal Assent on 5th August, 1891, having been approved by the Commons on 1st May 1891; it was the largest scheme to which parliamentary sanction in a single session had ever been given. The construction of the line was expected to take four years, with Bolsover Tunnel the longest work. The chairman was William Arkwright and the company engineer was Emmerson Bainbridge who was at the time M.P. for Gainsborough and managing director of the Bolsover Colliery Company.

Immediately the Railway Company had problems in raising the £5million capital required; its promoters had not met the subscription target and a decision was made in 1891 to construct the central section of the line from Chesterfield to Pyewipe junction near Lincoln. On 7th June 1892, Mrs Agnes Mary Arkwright, William's wife, cut the first sod on the site of the future Market Place station (which would provide spacious offices including the head office of the L.D. and E.C. Railway) at West Bars, Chesterfield, in front of distinguished guests and an immense, lively crowd. The privately owned Portland Hotel, still in existence, was built adjacent to the station and was officially opened in December 1899. Following the National Anthem Mrs Arkwright made a brief speech calling upon all those present to raise a cheer for the East to West Railway and was then congratulated by Mr A. Barnes and the Duke of Newcastle. She was presented with the barrow and spade with which she had performed the grass-cutting ceremony, then 300 guests were served a banquet in the beautifully decorated Memorial Hall.

However, the threat to William Arkwright's railway scheme caused him to resign as chairman in 1892, although remaining as a director and giving preference to Bainbridge (with his engineering experience) as the new chairman. The Great Eastern Railway, which saw little advantage in the east coast to west coast concept, offered financial help for the central section (which was under construction) and, in return, the L.D. and E.C. Railway agreed to abandon its plans for the west coast line from Chesterfield to the Manchester Ship Canal and to form a new company for the Pyewipe Junction (just north of Lincoln) to Sutton-on Sea route.

This plan never materialised; only the central section from Chesterfield to Lincoln (a distance of about 56 miles) was constructed and the eastern and western ends of the railway were not built; abandonment of the proposed route west of Chesterfield resulted in the Market Place Station becoming a terminus; (it was subsequently demolished in 1973). Arkwright's initial vision was ended and he resigned his directorship in 1896.

The L.D. and E.C. Railway therefore began at the Chesterfield Market Place Station: there were stations at Arkwright Town (the first stop) and Bolsover before entering the notorious Bolsover Tunnel which had problems of water seepage and mining subsidence; the line then passed through Scarcliffe Station then to Langwith Junction and into Nottinghamshire. The route of the L.D. and E.C. Railway took it across the natural contours of the area resulting in a number of cuttings, embankments, tunnels and viaducts being built.

Godfrey Downes-Rose, in his article 'Arkwright's Railway', explains that during the depression of the 1920s and 1930s day specials were held to the east coast resorts of Skegness, Cleethorpes and Mablethorpe, often arranged by local organisations. In ensuing years, several branch lines were built, connecting various collieries to the railway system and sometimes providing passenger services. For a long time the L.D. and E.C. Railway, before its final closure, had freight traffic even though passenger service declined; the passenger service was marketed as 'The Dukeries Route'.

In January 1907, the L.D. and E.C. Railway, after just 10 years of independent operation, during which time ordinary shareholders failed to receive any dividends, was absorbed by The Great Central Railway (the G.C.R.) which assumed control even though it had been particularly critical of the L.D. and E.C.'s original plans. Before then, work on the Arkwright Loop Line had begun; it left the L.D. and E.C. Railway to the east of Arkwright Town, went past the defunct Adelphi Iron Works, then westwards to join the Great Central Railway's Sheffield–Annesley main line with a stop at Spinkhill, the station for Mount St Mary's College.

The loop and main lines totally enclosed the village of Arkwright Town: as Godfrey Downes-Rose has observed, the development of the loop created a unique environment for the Arkwright Town residents; the main Chesterfield–Bolsover road, miners' allotments, football and cricket grounds, tennis areas and several fields belonging to Gorse Farm and the village were totally enclosed by railway lines. In the 1920s and 1930s the agricultural depression created neglected farmland through which the Great Central Railway's heavy goods trains passed. Zoe Elizabeth Hunter and Chris Booth have written excellent books which contain many photographs and track plans and are extremely detailed studies of the early years of the L.D. and E.C. Railway; many of the photographs indicate the visible remains of the railway.

9

Sutton Rock

One afternoon, during the school year 1953/54, three boys waited at the bus stop adjacent to St. Peter's Church, Calow, and across from the junior school which they attended. They were all friends from the same 'top class' (now Year 6) and one of the boys lived at Sutton Scarsdale: I was one of the two who had been invited for tea that day.

After alighting from the green, single-decker, Chesterfield Corporation bus we walked down the gentle slope of Rock Lane which eventually leads to Sutton Spring Wood, situated off the main road through Sutton Scarsdale and across from the entrance to the Hall drive. Walking past the three terraced houses situated on the left, known as 'Rock Cottages', into the dip at the bottom of the lane we clambered over a fence to the right into a small wood, crossed a stream and emerged from the trees on to a large, sloping lawn surrounded by rhododendrons. At the top of the rise stood a large mansion and I was amazed that a school friend should live in such a house. I still remember vividly that first view of the house and in particular the front entrance flanked by stone pillars and the windows across both floors of the front. The house was Sutton Rock.

We returned on subsequent occasions, rambling around the house and the adjoining barns and outbuildings which, on our visits, housed hundreds of turkeys. We roamed through family rooms as well as the empty, upper, second-storey rooms which had initially been the servants' quarters, opening windows to view the roof. We walked across fields to the railway line, watching steam trains travelling along the embankment of what I realised some years later was the Great Central Railway. After each visit and tea in the dining room we were taken home in our friend's father's Rover to our respective homes in Calow, in my case a terraced house on the main road, adjoining what was then the Co-operative store.

Sutton Rock (originally known as 'Sutton House') was an Italianate house possibly built between 1874 and 1876. The north side of the house, facing the lawn, had five bays and a central doorway; it was three bays deep and was probably built of top hard rock from the Wrang Quarry which had also provided stone to build the Hall. Sutton Rock was described in directories as 'a beautiful residence a short distance from Sutton Hall, built by William Arkwright Esq'.

It is not known who designed the house although, according to Maxwell Craven, it was possibly Thomas Flockton of Sheffield or Giles and Brookhouse, architects of Derby. A stables, coach house and offices of an earlier date suggest that Sutton Rock replaced a house of the late 18th century, or incorporated parts of it.

According to Walter Foulk's historical notes Sutton Rock was possibly built as a dower house for William's mother although she never lived there. It was probably built for William's oldest sister Fanny Elizabeth, who married Lieutenant-Colonel William Thornhill Blois, J.P., of Southwold, Suffolk in 1874. He was the brother of Sir John Ralph Blois, 8th Baronet of Cockfield Hall in Suffolk. William Blois had left the 14th Regiment of Foot before his marriage and in 1876 he joined the Warwickshire Militia as adjutant; he eventually retired from that regiment with the rank of lieutenant colonel.

William and Emily's first child, Geoffrey Stephen, was born in 1884 and three more sons followed in the next four years. In 1889 William died, aged 47, after taking his own life while visiting Bournemouth; he was possibly suffering from severe mental depression as the jury at the inquest found. By 1891 Emily and their four sons had vacated Sutton Rock and it was let in that year to A. Winter Barnes who stayed until 1895 when he and his wife moved to Eastbourne. In that year Sutton Rock was let to Charles Edward Stuart Cockburn and his wife Lilian, the daughter of Sir Molton Manningham-Buller, 2nd Baronet of Capesthorne. Charles Cockburn was the sub-agent to the Sutton Scarsdale Estate as well as being a J.P. and a Derbyshire County Alderman; he had been born in India in 1867 and was the grandson of Sir William Cockburn, 7th Baronet.

In 1910, Norman Connelly Robertson, the vicar of Sutton Scarsdale, conducted 40 baptisms and 22 burials, of which 16 were babies. He was instrumental in persuading Mrs Cockburn, who was similarly concerned by the high mortality rate of infants in Arkwright Town, to begin to raise sufficient funds by holding several activities at Sutton Rock, to pay a salary of £80 p.a. for the services of a district nurse. By 1912 it was possible to engage the services of a Nurse Tait and she lived at Nursery House, Arkwright. The Public House Trust, because of Cockburn's association with it, contributed £10 p.a. towards the nurse's salary.

By 1904 Charles Cockburn also had an address in London at 76 Jermyn Street and, because of his frequent absences from Sutton Scarsdale he resigned as Rector's Warden in 1914, having been warden for 14 years. He was also listed as a member of a number of prominent London clubs – Whites, Arthurs, Wellington and Automobile as well as the County club, Derby. In September 1917, the Cockburns left Sutton Rock intending to live at Godshill Park, Isle of Wight, but Charles died on 12th December 1917, at St James' Court, his latest London residence, before he could complete the move. The Revd. Robertson, vicar of Sutton Scarsdale, wrote that Charles Cockburn had been:

'... for so many years closely connected with Sutton church and the parish ... of a most generous nature, one could always feel assured of his willingness and readiness to help any good cause. He has left behind him a splendid example of patience in tribulation'.

Walter Foulk's notes, quoting the Revd. Robertson, give a positive summary of Charles Cockburn's character and achievements although there is no indication of the illness from which Cockburn had suffered for some years: 'The pluck and patience with which he met it was indeed astonishing. Before his illness 20 years ago you could not wish to see a finer specimen of a healthy, handsome man, and his batting and bowling feats for the old Sutton Scarsdale C.C. were things to be remembered. Since then it has been one long protracted struggle against the disease that robbed him of his once splendid physical powers. But there always remained within him the spirit of a lion as far as pluck and determination were concerned in facing his troubles.'

He was buried at Godshill Churchyard, in the parish which was to have been his future residence.

A memorial service was held at Christ Church, Lancaster Gate, at which Sir Frederick Bridge played *The Flowers of the Forest* and Chopin's *Funeral March*.

In September 1918, a legacy of £100 bequeathed by Charles Cockburn was left for the benefit of the deserving poor of the parish. The solicitors stated that:

'We fancy that your parish is in the happy position of not having any poor, but nevertheless, this legacy is payable'.

Sutton Rock was then uninhabited until it was sold at auction, as Lot 54, for £3,950 in the great estate sale of 6th November 1919, at the Market Hall in Chesterfield. The house was described in the sale catalogue as 'A Gentleman's Country Residence' of three floors, comprising an entrance hall, dining room, drawing room, morning room, library, conservatory and various servants' rooms and offices. It had nine bedrooms on the first floor and four on the second, together with main and secondary staircases as well as wine and beer cellars in the basement. Outside there was a range of buildings including stables, coach house, garage, cow house and pig cotes as well as gardens, lawns, trees, a tennis lawn and kitchen garden. The house, buildings and grounds were set in almost six acres; there were also over 16 acres of pasture land.

At the 1919 auction Sutton Rock was bought by the 9th Duke of Devonshire's estate, the date of conveyance being the 24th February 1920, and the Duke's land agent, Captain Joscelyn Dennis Penrose, J.P., was installed in the house. The Penrose family had originated in Ireland: the Revd. John Dennis Penrose (1804-1904) and his wife produced eight children, the oldest of whom was James Edward; he trained in Dublin as a land agent, beginning the family's lengthy association with the Devonshire estates. After managing the Devonshire estates in Ireland and living in a wing of Lismore Castle, County Waterford, James (1850–1936) retired in the early 1930s. His son, Joscelyn Dennis, the oldest of six children, became a pupil land agent on the Chatsworth estate by 1911 but at the onset of World War One served in Alexandria as a captain.

He moved to Sutton Rock in 1920 to become the Duke's land agent for the Hardwick Estate which he managed until 1948 when he retired, moving with his wife to Oxfordshire. Captain Penrose died in 1978 aged 96.

Captain Penrose had married Edith Florence Preston in 1913 and they had a daughter, Ruth Esme, born in 1915 and a son, John Dennis Fitzgerald, born in 1919. Ruth married Hugo Read who, after a career as a prep-schoolmaster, became a pupil land agent and was appointed to land agency posts in Nottingham and Graythwaite between 1938 and 1946. From 1946 he became the deputy land agent for Hardwick, taking full responsibility from 1948 as well as for the Buxton estates from the early 1950's. He then became the sole agent for all the Derbyshire Estates from the mid-1950s until 1973. He trained his successor, Derrick Penrose (nephew of Captain Penrose) as a pupil land agent at Hardwick in the early 1950s; Derrick, who had married Zoe Becher, then worked with Hugo as a Deputy Agent at Chatsworth until 1973 when he became chief land agent until the 1990s when he retired.

During the occupation of Sutton Rock by Captain and Mrs Penrose the gardens were open to the public from 2–7pm, admission 3d, under the National Garden Scheme which operated in the late 1930s and early 1940s. A total of 28 gardens were open at different times between April and September in aid of the Derbyshire County Nursing Association: the day for visiting the Sutton Rock garden was Sunday, 3rd May. Examples of other Derbyshire houses involved in the scheme were Chatsworth House, Thornbridge Hall, Hassop Hall, Lea Hurst, Melbourne Hall, Osmaston Manor, Clay Cross Hall, Walton Lodge, Hardwick Hall (House and Garden), Holbrook Hall, Alton Manor, Tissington Hall, Sudbury Hall and Parwich Hall.

Life at Sutton Rock has been given historical significance by Ruth Read, who spent the first three years of her life living in a wing of Lismore Castle while her father was abroad during World War One. After living at The Grange at Hardwick for a couple of years the move to Sutton Rock took place and Ruth Read's writing, provided by her daughter, Susan Watts, gives a wonderful insight into life at Sutton Rock and is a reminder of a world that is rapidly disappearing. Extracts from Ruth's memoirs, written in 1990, constitute a valid historical document:

'Sometime around 1920 when I was about five it was decided that Sutton Rock, which had been the Dower House for Sutton Hall, should be purchased by the Estate to be the family home of my father Captain Joscelyn Denis Penrose, who was His Grace's land agent for the Hardwick Estate. Soon after my parents, my baby brother John and I had moved in I can remember running around the very big garden and all outbuildings and feeling like everything was a great new adventure. It was to be my home until I left to get married in October 1939. My parents left Sutton when my father retired in 1948.

Sutton Rock had very big high rooms and enormous plate glass windows. There were four big reception rooms on the ground floor, four large bedrooms and the nursery quarters on the first floor where John and I spent most of our time with Nanny, as well as extensive staff quarters. When we first moved in there was only about enough furniture from our previous home, The Grange at Hardwick, to properly furnish two rooms so we very much rattled about in the house until more furniture arrived in 1922 from my grandparents' family home in Ireland that had been closed down. In the mornings we were sent into the garden to play, (most often later to squabble and fight), and every day, rain or shine we went on a walk with Nanny, usually to Heath where she would hold a long boring conversation with Mrs Hardwick, keeper of the village shop. We would then have to hurry back home to be in time for tea in the nursery at 4.30pm. We were then dressed in our best clothes and delivered to the drawing room where we played 'Snakes and Ladders' or whatever with our parents. Promptly at 6pm Nanny would collect us for bath and bed before they changed to be ready for dinner at home, entertaining guests or going out. That routine continued until John went away to prep. school.

There was a large 'Eagle' cooking range in the kitchen. It also heated the water and was purported to consume a ton of coal each week (free to the Duke as a Coal Owner, but then only 10/- per ton to buy) The kitchen quarters lay along a dark tiled passage which had a row of mechanical bells along the top of one wall and festoons of unlagged lead piping. Next to the kitchen was the scullery, a dreadful place with a big flat stone sink and a barred window which looked out onto a thicket of dark evergreens. I don't think the sun ever got into it and it had no heating so the scullery maid must have been frozen in winter. The parlour maid's pantry next to it, lined with cupboards for china and silver, was almost as bad. On the other side of the passage were the pretty spartan staff sitting room, a narrow room used for cleaning knives and shoes, an enormous double larder with stone shelves and the provisions store cupboard. There was usually the lovely smell of freshly baked bread which was stored in big earthenware pancheons with cloths over their tops. Eggs from the chickens, kept in the outbuildings behind the stables, were preserved in waterglass in big earthenware crocks in the larder.

Some steps led down from the draughty door at the far end of the passage into a small yard. On one side was the wash house and laundry where there were two large coppers for boiling the linen. The fires underneath them had to be lit early on washdays ready for when a woman used to come each week. There was a long scrubbed wooden table down one side of the laundry on which the ironing was done with flat irons. On the third side of this yard was a building housing the acetylene gas plant which provided the lighting for the house till the late 1920s when the estate arranged to have an electricity supply laid on from Staveley Works. Unfortunately as it was a 30-cycle supply some appliances would not work unless their motors were rewound.

The live-in staff at Sutton Rock consisted of a cook, kitchen maid, housemaid and parlourmaid in addition to Nanny. The kitchen maid's salary was about 7/6d a week, plus keep of course. Cook would have earned about £1. The services of gardener Oakley and chauffeur/handyman Parker came with the job as did free coal, electricity, car, repairs, decorating and telephone but my father's salary never reached £1000 a year even up to his retirement in 1948. Nanny's salary was £50 a year. Both Oakley and Parker lived in houses provided for them in the village; both were beyond excellence at their jobs.

The small yard led into the large paved stable yard at the far end of which was the old coach house. Soon after the family had moved to Sutton Rock and the Estate Office was also moved across from Hardwick into three upstairs rooms in this building. This arrangement did not last long and the office had been moved to St Helen's Street, Chesterfield by 1925. The lower part of the coach house had been turned into a garage that at a pinch, could house three cars and Parker's motorbike and sidecar. This was his domain where he kept the cars in superb order, doing virtually all the repairs himself. He washed them every day if they had been used. A probably highly dangerous petrol supply kept in maybe 100 two gallon cans was stored in a building behind it, next to the one that housed the chickens. 'Charlie' Parker could mend anything and make anything out of nothing with perfect workmanship. He had been gassed in the First War and died comparatively young during the second. He was a rebel at heart but I'm sure totally loyal to us.

Oakley managed the entire garden single handed though how he did it I don't know as it covered about four to five acres including a two acre field at the bottom where he had originally planted two tons of daffodil bulbs for the previous owner. In our time it was in its glory, enhanced by masses of shrubs planted to my mother's design and much to her credit. People would walk several miles when it was opened to the public each spring in aid of the District Nurses' Fund. There was also a rose garden enclosed in a circular clipped yew hedge which was a real sun trap in summer. There were a lot of nice trees and shrubs in the rest of the garden and I am always taken straight back there in memory when I smell the perfume of azaleas in spring or a balsam poplar in the sun.

On the bottom lawn were three large Lebanon Cedars under whose branches we would 'play houses'. There was also a long snake-shaped flower bed all along the side of the drive which had to be bedded out with over 2000 plants over twice a year (wall flowers in spring and antirrhinums in summer) in addition to a large greenhouse, a conservatory and a big kitchen garden. My mother had a big rock garden which she looked after herself. On the top lawn were two tennis courts which were the focus for a series of tennis parties each summer.

There was a rigid protocol in the domestic scene. We were Miss Ruth and Master John and they to us were Mr Oakley, Mrs Buchanan etc. unless they were young when their Christian names could be used. Amongst themselves similar rules applied and bitter jealousies arose. Nanny was once heard to remark to some clearly 'inferior' nanny "We breathe the same air as Dukes and Duchesses". At one time during the early 1920s Oakley's daughter in law was also employed and made a very good governess for us. She shared lunch in the nursery with us but was despised and kept firmly in her place by Nanny who also despised the cooks, at least one of whom gave notice because of her outspoken criticism.

Undue fraternisation was frowned upon and we had to make our visits to the garage or potting shed surreptitiously to talk with Oakley or Parker from whom in fact we received some of our most valuable education and knowledge of the real world. Parker later taught me to drive before my 16th birthday, the first lessons involving me changing gear at the appropriate moment from the passenger seat while he doubled declutched. He also taught me the basics of vehicle maintenance, changing a wheel etc.

Being far from the shops my mother had a large store cupboard so that we could be self-sufficient although meat and milk were delivered to the house. It was unlocked every Thursday morning when all the maids had to hand in a list of what they needed to last the week. Each year she made a huge order for Harrods sale which would arrive in late January in a large crate. It always included a hundredweight of yellow household soap as long bars which had to be cut up by hand. It was one of my jobs to do that with an old kitchen knife and resulted in two very sore hands. The soap was stored on the top of the airing cupboard for a year so that it would get hard and not melt so quickly.

My mother also made a weekly state shopping visit to Chesterfield driven by Parker. She never learned to drive and was always nervous being driven having been involved in earlier accidents. There was usually no difficulty in parking within a few yards of any shop, if not right in front of it so she would go to Boots library to change her books and deal with such personal matters as buying toilet paper at Dutton's the other chemist. There she was always attended by Mr Dutton himself, the order given and acknowledged in whispers, the articles retrieved from the stock room, held behind his back, wrapped up in secretive haste and sealed with red sealing wax. Meanwhile Parker would have collected the groceries etc. which she had ordered in advance by telephone.

The village was very small and strung out. The Post Office was originally on the road to Arkwright Town, kept by Mrs Cheetham. As a great treat she would give us children a glass of ice cold water from her well on the opposite side of the road. After her death the PO was moved to a cottage opposite the bottom end of our daffodil field and run by Mrs Hatton and later by the wife of our gardener Cragg who succeeded Oakley. Mr & Mrs Bacon, owners of a garage in Hasland, lived a little further up the lane. They had a very gifted daughter Katie who became a concert pianist and married an American Professor of Music in New York.

Mother was very active in the local Mothers' Union and belonged to the 'Linen League' which raised funds for the Chesterfield Hospital. During the war she did a lot of welfare work in Arkwright Town where there was much need for it. She told of one visit to a family (13 children) on baking day when the two youngest (twins) were sitting almost naked in a large pancheon of dough which was set to rise in front of the fire. She was amazed when another of the village ladies and wife of a minor colliery official who had come into a large legacy spent it building a new detached house at the end of the row she had previously lived in. My father was also popular there and they had the honour of one of the three rows being renamed Penrose Street. All the Sutton children walked the 2½ miles to school there and he often scooped them up in the car on his way home, earning him the name 't' Sutton Bus'.

Tragically a few years after my father's retirement when the estate sold the house, it was resold for open cast coal extraction and house, garden and trees were demolished and now only two stone gateposts remain as monuments to the beauty that was there and the pleasure and civilisation that we had from it.'

Wendie Lee also has memories of her father's employment at Sutton Rock: about 1941 Minnie and Walter Lee, with their daughter Wendie moved to Sutton Scarsdale. Her father Walter was employed by Capt. Penrose as a gardener and chauffeur, living in ... 'the third cottage down Rock Lane and next to the field. It was called 'Rock Cottage. At the bottom left hand corner of the field was a large garden where dad grew flowers and vegetables for the Rock and for his own family use. He also tended the garden at the house. At the bottom of the field on the lane was another house – the village post office owned by Mr Cragg'

Wendie has fond memories of running down the lane with a letter to Mr Cragg to buy a stamp and put it on the letter while her mum waited for her at the cottage. Next door, in the middle cottage, lived Mr and Mrs Dobson, who had a son.

'Mrs Penrose spent a lot of time at our house – Mum and she were good friends and Mrs Penrose had a cute dog'.

When Wendie was three years old Judith was born (in 1943); Mrs Penrose often came to see Judith and walked down the lane with Minnie and Wendie. Wendie also remembers going across the lane with her dad and to the big house, into the kitchens and seeing lots of maids in black dresses with white aprons and hats. Wendie's father, Walter, used to take her to the kitchen gardens for the Rock.

Capt. and Mrs Penrose left Sutton Scarsdale about 1945–6: they were moving to Oxfordshire and Minnie didn't want to leave the area so Walter gave up his job and they moved to a farm in Pilsley: Wendie has very fond memories of living there.

Ruth's reminiscences, written in 1990, and Wendie's recent memoirs provided by her daughter, Faye Hall, bring Sutton Rock and its inhabitants and staff back to life, as well as giving a glimpse of what life would have been like at the Hall.

Mr and Mrs Walter Foulk bought Sutton Rock, 16¾ acres of farm land, a full range of outbuildings and the 'three Rock Cottages' (one with vacant possession) for a total of £3,900. Approximately 14½ out of the 16¾ acres had been requisitioned by the Ministry of Food and Power for open-casting. Mr and Mrs Foulk had already run, since 1943, an extensive accredited poultry farm at New Whittington but had decided to move because, with four children, they needed extra accommodation. Already the managing director of the Chesterfield Poultry Producers at Duckmanton Mr Foulk anticipated selecting birds from the New Whittington farm to form the basis of their stock at Sutton Scarsdale before selling up: Sutton Rock would therefore be the headquarters of a large-scale poultry farm and this was certainly the situation when I used to visit.

Mr Foulk died in 1956 and eventually Mrs Foulk and the family moved away.

Sutton Rock was acquired by the British Coal Board who unceremoniously demolished it in or about 1964 to allow open cast coal mining operations. The site which Sutton Rock occupied is now owned by Mr David Sewell of Palterton Hall.

10

The 1919 Sale

The first sale of the Sutton Scarsdale Estate took place on the 31st July and the 1st August 1919. The auction items were the ... 'Surplus Furnishings and Outdoor Effects in and about Sutton Scarsdale Hall ...' and the auctioneers were Henry Spencer and Sons of Retford. On the first day lots 1–479 were auctioned, comprising outdoor effects (lots 1–72) such as lawn mowers, garden chairs, fencing, timber, gates, vases, plant stands, a dog cart, tree transplanting machine and a railway carriage. Poultry appliances (lots 73–97) offered examples such as several large portable poultry houses, show pens, show baskets, bench, table and sundries. Kennel appliances (lots 98–125) comprising several dog sleeping benches, dog kennel, dog travelling box, benches, cupboards, chest of drawers, large tool chest and other items which were auctioned.

The remaining lots up to and including no. 479 offered a complete variety of items from the kitchen, larder, servants' hall, lamp hall, boot hall, scullery, laundry, servants' small hall, butler's room, dessert room, butler's pantry, butler's bedroom, store room, cellar, fishing room, gun room, housemaid's pantry and cupboard, landing, bathroom and bedrooms 1–16, including the dressing room adjoining Bedroom No. 1.

On the second day lots 480–876 offered china, ornaments and bric-a-brac and 'silver plated goods' as well as the contents of the entrance hall and lounge, dining room, small drawing room, drawing room, smoking room, library (downstairs) and library (upstairs), ballroom, inner hall, Bathroom No. 2, landing over front hall, staircase and landing, landing and Bedrooms Nos. 17 to 33. A very small example of items sold is as follows:

Lot Number	Description of Item	Price Paid
263 (Butler's Bedroom)	Painted chest of five drawers.	£2.15s.0d
331 (Bedroom No.1)	Excellent painted wardrobe with sliding shelves, cupboards and drawers.	£5.15s.0d
355 (Bedroom No. 2)	Suite in pitch pine comprising; - Large wardrobe, Duchesse dressing table with swing glass, marble top wash-stand, and towel rail.	£27.10s.0d
408 (Bedroom No. 9)	Mahogany dressing table.	£2.12s.6d
448 (Cupboard)	Copper warming pan.	£1.10s.0d
573 (Entrance Hall and Lounge)	640 super feet of handsomely carved oak panelling including pair of book-cases of 60 square feet, each with brass drop handles.	£60.5s.0d
576 (Entrance Hall and Lounge)	Boudoir' Grand Pianoforte by Gustav Hagspiel, Dresden, in burr walnut case, in excellent condition.	£90.0s.0d
577 (Entrance Hall and Lounge)	Piano stool	£2.5s.0d
597 (Entrance Hall and Lounge)	Wall clock	10s.0d
610 (Dining Room)	Set of six exceedingly well-made solid mahogany chairs in red Russian leather, with hair-stuffed seats.	£32.6s.0d
611 (Dining Room)	Set of six ditto	£40.0s.0d
612 (Dining Room)	Set of six ditto	£42.6s.0d

666 (Ball Room)	Fine set of 12 oak tall back Dutch chairs, beautifully carved and in good preservation.	£36.0s.0d
684 (Inner Hall)	Fine old carved Chippendale side table with marble top, 2ft. 8in. by 5ft. 8in.	£13.10s.0d

The sale of the Sutton Scarsdale freehold landed estate took place at the Chesterfield Market Hall on Thursday, 6th November 1919. The auctioneers were Thurgood and Martin of London and the solicitors, also of London, were Treherne, Higgins and Co. Within the Parishes of Sutton-cum-Duckmanton, Staveley, Heath, Temple Normanton, Calow, Bolsover and Scarcliffe, the estate, approximately 5,176 acres in area, consisted of 33 farms, 19 smallholdings, 70 dwelling houses including a 'comfortable family residence', a licensed house, shops, cottages and building land, as well as Sutton Scarsdale Hall, a 'Stately Historical Mansion with Beautiful Gardens and well Timbered Deer Park'. According to the 8th November 1919 edition of *The Derbyshire Times*, the interest in the sale was massive and the Market Hall was packed with potential buyers, many of them already tenants of the estate.

Before the auction, William Arkwright, the owner of the estate, had given specific instructions that the estate be allotted in the smallest possible lots so that the tenants might have the opportunity of purchasing the holdings that they occupied. To make it easier for tenants to do so William had arranged that they could leave 60 per cent of the purchase money on mortgage at 5 per cent. To a round of enthusiastic applause the auctioneer explained, to much further applause, that tenants were to have the opportunity in any sale as a way of rejecting any offers from speculators to buy, for example, half a property. It was reported that William Arkwright hoped that there would be nothing in the conduct of the sale to interfere with tenants purchasing their lots.

Examples of tenants who purchased their holdings were Mr W. A. Bennett who took Lot 2 – Inkersall Farm, Staveley, with three stone-built cottages and 232 acres of land for £4,800; Mr William Elliott (Lot 12) – a smallholding at Middle Duckmanton and five acres for £850; Mr F. Holmes (Lot 13) - Sutton Mill Farm with 136 acres for £2,900; Mr R.

Cowlishaw (Lot 27) – a house with blacksmith's shop and one acre for £400. With old brickworks, two cottages and 51 acres, the site of the Adelphi Ironworks known as Works Farm (Lot 34) was bought by William Spooner (tenant of the farm) for £900. He also purchased three freehold cottages (Lot 35) at Works Farm for £240. Owlcotes Farm (Lot 49) at Heath situated on the site of Oldcotes, built by Bess of Hardwick with over 322 acres, was sold to Mr G. T. Welch, the tenant, for £4,000. The house and smithy at Calow (Lot 82) with over four acres were bought by the tenant, Mr A. Smith.

Sutton Scarsdale Hall, as Lot 37, with over 593 acres which included the deer park, plantation and grounds was withdrawn at £12,600 after bidding began at £8,000. Sutton Rock, Lot 54, with over 23 acres of land, was purchased for £3,950 on behalf of the 9th Duke of Devonshire. The Staveley Coal and Iron Company purchased six farms for £11,950 and the Brampton Brewery Company, who already tenanted the 'Arkwright Arms' Hotel (Lot 24), bought it for £3,600. Duckmanton Lodge, (Lot 74), with over three acres, the historic home built by the Smith family who had operated the Adelphi Ironworks, was bought by the tenant, Mr D. N. Turner, for £2,000: he also bought two acres of building land opposite Duckmanton Lodge for £280 as well as two semi-detached cottages (Lot 79) nearby for £300.

At the 1919 sale, when the Temple Normanton part of the Sutton Scarsdale estate was sold off in lots, the ancient manor, tracing its origins back to the Elizabethan period, ceased to exist as a single area in the hands of one owner. The manor of Temple Normanton, originally of 514 acres, consisted of about 230 acres in 1919, several buildings and parcels of land having been sold off over the centuries which had led to an increase in the number of small landowners in the village. According to Peter and Janet Wright, when the Sutton Scarsdale estate was auctioned, the sale included a large proportion of the village – Hill Farm (Lot 62), Church Farm (Lot 66), a number of smallholdings, houses and cottages, land, the Co-op shop on Mansfield Road as well as the freehold ground rent of the Wesleyan Mission chapel.

Several tenants were able to buy the property they were renting, as William Arkwright wished: for example, the Corbriggs smallholding (Lot

64) and four acres were sold for £395 to Miss A Farnsworth, the tenant who also bought (Lot 65) a cottage at Corbriggs with one acre. Mr J. Marriott bought Church Farm, Mr E. Cooper bought a smallholding and gardens and Miss E. Watson bought the house (Lot 69) known as Church Villa. The remaining lots were purchased by the Grassmoor Colliery Co., the Hasland Cooperative Society, and a minority of miscellaneous individuals. Of the 102 lots for sale, 15 lots were either withdrawn or were listed as 'not offered' or 'No Lot'. All other lots which sold on the day, mostly to tenants, realised a total amount of £101,817.

On Tuesday, October 19th and Wednesday, October 20th, 1920, the remaining contents of the Hall were auctioned on the premises by Hampton and Sons of Pall Mall, London. The first day saw the sale of 'A Collection of Pictures of Sporting Dogs, Portraits, Old Sporting and Theatrical Prints, 18th Century Mezzo-tints and library of Miscellaneous Literature'. Many old Prints, (Lots 65–124), chiefly of sporting interest were followed by mostly theatrical portraits, many of them relating to the Kemble family.

A library of over 4,000 volumes, comprising lots 130–374, was then auctioned: classic works were offered, including complete sets of history, biography, voyages and travels, drama, poetry, natural history, 'Standard English and French Authors' by authors such as Sir Walter Scott, Thomas Bewick, Edward Gibbon, The Earl of Chesterfield, Samuel Johnson, Daniel Defoe, Lord Byron, Charles Dickens, Thomas Carlyle, William Shakespeare, Lord Tennyson, Voltaire, John Milton, Charles Darwin, Clarendon, William Wordsworth and many others.

On the second day, 'Garden Ornaments, Entrance Gates and Outdoor Effects' which included a 1920 Ruston-Hornsby five-seater touring car, the antique ornamental wrought iron entrance gates (gates were 10ft. 9ins. wide, overall 20ft. 8ins. wide, posts 8ft. 3ins. high) were sold. Examples of items from bedrooms were bedsteads, mirrors, oak chests, wardrobes, mattresses and washstands. The sale of silver (lots 551–610) comprised hundreds of items such as sets of cutlery, table knives, kettles, jugs, candlesticks, mugs, dishes, cruets, teapots and candelabrums.

The examples listed are but a small representation of the many items sold on the various auction days, but they give an indication of the different articles collectively used daily by the Hall's residents, visitors and staff when the Hall was functioning like any other great country house. The number and type of rooms listed in the auction catalogues also give a good indication of the size of the Hall and the necessary servants' rooms as well as those available to the Arkwright family.

My own specific links to the Hall are two books (Childe Harold's Pilgrimage and other poems), safely located on my bookshelves, both by Lord Byron and respectively published in 1812 and 1816, the earlier one of which contains Robert Arkwright's bookplate. These were given to me by a fellow member of the Arkwright Society and they must be representative of the many articles obtained at the 1919/1920 auctions and which are still present in many homes throughout the country or abroad, and which still exist as mementos of the Hall in its Georgian, Victorian and Edwardian heyday.

34. The Hall Pine Room reconstructed and used in the 1945 film *Kitty*

35. The Hall Pine Room reconstructed and used in the 1945 film *Kitty*

36. The Hall Pine Room reconstructed and used in the 1945 film *Kitty*

37. Image of re-constructed first Oak Room (Philadelphia Museum of Art)

38. Image of re-constructed second Oak Room (Philadelphia Museum of Art)

39. Lithograph of Frances Arkwright, ordered by the 6th Duke on her death in 1849

40. William Arkwright

41. Agnes Arkwright

42. Pointer dog outside Thorn House

43. A lady, (possibly Agnes Arkwright) with pointer dog in front of Trentham Vase at Thorn

44. 'Sea Breeze' William Arkwright's pointer dog

11

Conclusion

Many documents of different types exist relating to the sale of the various lots of the Sutton Scarsdale estate; inspection reports, sale prices of different lots, particulars of conditions of sale, particulars of properties, agreements, payment and receipts, agendas for meetings as well as various letters to individuals or groups of individuals. According to an inspection report by Frederic A. Walker, dated 9th March 1921, there was a considerable amount of small timber and some 'fairly good-sized timber in the 190 acres of Sutton Spring Wood'. Over three acres of Sutton Spring Wood came up the west side of Sutton Lane, near Oaktree Farm. On the east side of Sutton Lane, Kennell's Plantation contained over nine acres and the Cockburn Plantation nearly 19 acres. According to the report there was 'remarkably good timber in the deerpark, some trees having fine girth'. There was also a very fine avenue – 'the trees were very good although old'.

Kelly's 1922 *Directory of Derbyshire* describes Sutton Scarsdale Hall as 'a splendid edifice of the Corinthian order ... it is now unoccupied'. Presumably the Hall, which had been withdrawn at the 1919 auction, was still untouched and in its original condition in 1922; this is borne out by James Austin's diary, extracts of which are as follows:

2nd January 1922 – put new lock on Sutton Hall.

31st August 1922 – went to Sutton Hall to photograph the staircase.

A report dated 21st September 1922, by Wilcockson and Cutts, Architects of Knifesmith Gate, Chesterfield, discussed the best procedure for the possible dismantling of the Hall, together with the eventual conversions of the brewhouse (sometimes referred to as 'the Old Priory') and stables. After careful consideration, the architects suggested that the whole of the walls of the Hall should be left standing as the labour involved would cost too much and that the walls could be sold if any road-making was to be done in the nearby vicinity. All doors, fireplaces, cupboards, shutters etc. should be taken out of each room during the winter months and left loose in each respective room until the following spring, then parcelled into small lots and sold by auction outside. This suggested method, according to the report, would prevent would-be purchasers from having access all over the Hall and pulling down material and taking away items which did not belong to them. Some of the wall panelling was to be sold privately, in position, in the relevant rooms, as this was seen to be the better way of dealing with it: the main and secondary staircases were to be sold.

The most valuable asset was said to be the lead on the roof and cornices, an estimated weight, after careful measurement, of 50 to 60 tons or more, and saleable at about £22 per ton. It was suggested that it was of the 'cast' kind and should be sold to a large lead-dealing firm by the weighed ton because of the possibility that the weight could have been in excess of the estimated amount. The value of the material from the dismantling of the Hall was estimated to be approximately £1,750 although that figure was dependent upon who actually did the dismantling as well as a considerable amount of work being done with regard to the maintenance and disposal of the material.

The brewhouse was probably initially built as a 16th century barn then remodeled to four almshouses in the 17th century then to a brewhouse in the 18th century to allow beer to be piped underground to the Hall. It was in good condition at the time of the report and it was proposed to convert it into two houses, each possessing three or four acres of land, one house fronting towards the east and the other facing west. The estimated cost of converting was approximately £500. It was proposed to convert the stables into eight or nine cottages having four or five acres of land each, and one farmhouse: the estimated cost of this conversion was approximately £1,300.

An alternative proposal in the report was to sell the brewhouse and stables as they stood, after carefully setting the boundaries. The report concluded that the owners should meet and settle the procedure to be taken 'as there appears to be no advantage in postponing the breaking-up of the Hall'.

The Hall was eventually sold in the early 1920s, possibly for £5,000, to Haslam Builders Limited, a consortium of Chesterfield builders and contractors whose agent was Mr James Austin, the under-manager of the Grassmoor Colliery, near Chesterfield. James Austin, of Rose Cottage Grassmoor, Tom Wilson Austin of Shepherdswell, Dover (mining engineer,) Tom Smeaton Wilcockson, (architect) and Frederic Arthur Walker of Chesterfield (solicitor) had formed a syndicate who purchased the unsold portions of the estate, including Sutton Scarsdale Hall.

Unable to find a purchaser, Haslam Builders decided to dismantle the Hall: according to Richard Sheppard, their interest was in building materials and particularly the extensive stonework and timber work in the structure. Most of the stone from the outbuildings was recycled as well as nearly all the Hall's timbers; massive wooden joists were taken in order to build houses in various parts of Chesterfield, including Brampton and Somersall.

The grand staircase and Adam fireplaces, which were beautifully and elaborately inlaid with Blue John, as well as panelling from three of the Hall's rooms, were purchased by Charles Lockhart Roberson of Knightsbridge, a London dealer who sold many English country house rooms and fittings to American collectors. They were then sold in 1928 to Fiske Kimball, the director of the Philadelphia Museum of Art, where they are still on display, although the panelling from Sutton Scarsdale Hall was modified and possibly added to in order to be accommodated into the rooms of the Philadelphia Museum. The interiors are impressive, richly panelled and carved, with marble fireplaces, but according to Donna Corbin, the associate curator for European decorative art at the museum, probably no whole room came from Sutton Scarsdale Hall. Although authentic elements from Sutton Scarsdale Hall do exist in the rooms, Kimball wanted a setting for the museum's collection of English paintings and other furnishings.

One of the Sutton Scarsdale Hall rooms, the No. 4 Pine Room, was purchased by the newspaper entrepreneur William Randolph Hearst, but stayed in its packing case in one of his warehouses in New York until it was sold, because of financial difficulties, in the 1940s to Paramount Film Studios. In 1945 the room was used as a film set for the film *Kitty* made at Paramount Studios, in 1945; it won an Oscar for the best film set at the Academy Awards of 1946. The room was donated in 1954 to the Huntingdon Library, a museum in Pasadena, Los Angeles, where it remains today.

In 1985 two chairs of outstanding quality, originally made by Thomas Howe of Westminster, and part of a suite of two settees, two footstools and 12 chairs probably commissioned for Sutton Scarsdale Hall during, or shortly after 1724, were sold to the Leeds Art Gallery for £39,000. The whole suite had been exported to France soon after 1900 then part of it was destroyed by fire in Brussels in 1910. The remainder of the suite was exported to New York where other items were lost in a fire. Only seven original chairs and one footstool survived. The Metropolitan Museum of New York owns two chairs and a footstool: the Frick collection in New York possesses two chairs and the Cooper Heart Museum in Washington has a single chair.

A similar situation had arisen at Wingerworth Hall, situated a few miles from Sutton Scarsdale: the Hall had also been designed by Francis Smith of Warwick, was built between 1726 and 1729 for Sir Thomas Windsor Hunloke who had inherited a fortune from his mother, Catherine Throckmorton, and put up for sale in May 1920. The Hall and 260 acres did not sell and in June, at a second auction, it was still not sold.

Eventually W. M. Twigg and Sons of Matlock bought it for demolition: Mr David Allen, a descendant of the Twigg family and a representative of the current firm of W. M. Twigg and Sons has confirmed that his family firm were involved in the sale and demolition of Wingerworth Hall but not of Sutton Scarsdale Hall. Wingerworth Hall was demolished in 1921 but only part of the south-west and north-west wings, initially serving as kitchens, offices and servants' quarters now remain; they were saved for conversion and are privately occupied today.

The owner of the 5,340 acre Wingerworth estate, Major Philip

Hunloke, had inherited it in 1904 and as a sailing master to George V, in charge of the Royal Yacht, had other interests and responsibilities. As with the Sutton Scarsdale estate and many others throughout the country the Wingerworth estate had become heavily mortgaged and it was not uncommon for many estates, no longer a regular and reliable source of income after World War One, to be offered for sale. Just under a third of the Wingerworth estate lots were bought by Hunloke tenants: many local non-tenants as well as those from a greater distance bought portions of the estate. As with Sutton Scarsdale Hall, several rooms from Wingerworth Hall were sold to Roberson's of Knightsbridge, as well as a room to William Randolph Hearst which was not used and eventually sold to a Dallas architect. Oak panelling, doors and a fireplace from one of the rooms was sold to the St. Louis Art Museum in Missouri but, like the Sutton Scarsdale Hall rooms in Philadelphia, had to be modified to fit the exhibition room.

Sometime after 1920 the Sitwells, who had a long-standing, social relationship with the Arkwrights, became involved with the ruins of Sutton Scarsdale Hall. Sacheverell Sitwell while living at Renishaw Hall and 'recovering from a long illness' received word that he and his brother had better go to Sutton Scarsdale. Sacheverell responded by travelling to Sutton Scarsdale Hall with Sir Osbert to find that architectural damage had been done; the interior of the Hall was gutted and in a ruinous state. Sacheverell's account of their visit, recorded in his *'British Architects and Craftsmen'*, is as follows:

'Sutton Scarsdale is a … building with a Corinthian, stone facade, of supreme elegance by Smith of Warwick, architect of Stoneleigh Abbey. No purchaser would even buy the stone, and, later, it was proposed to blow it up with gunpowder. It contained a stair, with twisted balusters, and some splendid panelled rooms which have been removed to an American museum. But the glory of Sutton Scarsdale was in the pair of Venetian saloons, on two floors, one above another, with fireplaces at each end; all, fireplaces, walls, and ceilings, the work of Artari "gentleman plasterer", as he is called by Gibbs. When we saw it, the ceiling of the lower room had fallen in, so that there was the extraordinary spectacle of four Venetian mantelpieces, all of the richest work imaginable, richer, far, than anything in a Venetian palace, hanging in the air, with the remains of the coloured stucco in panels and niches upon the walls, and some fragments of the figures on the higher stucco ceiling.

One of the mantelpieces ... in the upper saloon was still perfect, and we were told that an offer of ten shillings would be accepted for it. But some days went by before a farm cart could be sent over to fetch it, and during that interval it had collapsed entirely and lay in little pieces on the floor.

Such was the fate of what was, certainly, the finest work of Artari or either of the Italians in England for, in other houses, at Houghton or at Mereworth, they had to show restraint and work up to the full Palladian solemnity of their setting. Only at Sutton Scarsdale was it the full Venetian Rococo, and here, perhaps, at greater outlay than any Venetian family ... could afford'.

The story of the destruction of Sutton Scarsdale Hall was, according to Sacheverell, 'an extraordinary instance of what has been allowed to happen under our eyes, by way of destruction of our national heritage of works of art with no redress, and no means of prevention'. In 1942 the artist John Piper was staying at Renishaw Hall: he was a long-standing associate of the Sitwell family and was always looked upon with affection, especially by Edith and Osbert. Piper always referred to Sir Osbert as his 'patron' and Sir Osbert had a great interest for John Piper's paintings, demanding new ones regularly.

John painted many pictures of Renishaw Hall, Bolsover Castle, Sutton Scarsdale Hall, Hardwick Hall and other buildings. His diary entry for 15th November 1942, describes his first visit to Sutton Scarsdale Hall:

'...to Sutton Scarsdale, through Arkwrightstown [sic]. Curious slightly suburban atmosphere of Sutton Scarsdale, owing probably to its last business-man [colliery manager] owner. Elders rioting in de-leafed condition. Dark, reddish, pinkish, but not rich in colour and not light and pale and sky-ridden like Bolsover. Becoming very ruinous'.

According to Alexandra Harris, in *Romantic Moderns*, John Piper 'was at his most receptive in this exposed, scarred countryside. Upon his return home he wrote that':

"I got home after, with my head full of blank-trunked trees, scythed grass, the tumbled beauty of Renishaw Park, Bolsover in the mist, Sutton Scarsdale in drizzle and Barlborough in fitful sun".

Sir Osbert, together with the writers George Orwell, Evelyn Waugh and Graham Greene had a common horror of the violated landscape and the lost beauty of 18th century estates. In 1945, in the first volume *Left Hand, Right Hand!* of his autobiography, Sir Osbert Sitwell wrote that:

'Sutton Scarsdale, with its grand facade, Corinthian columns and elaborate coat-of-arms, was, at the time of which I write, still lived in, whereas today it has been reduced by the greed of the native speculator to an eyeless and roofless ruin in which the foxes nest, and from which they have to be dislodged before a hunt. Today even the lake is sightless and lies drained'.

In 1946, Sir Osbert, having conversed with Harold Taylor, the Sutton Scarsdale churchwarden, and realising that the Hall was threatened with demolition because of its deterioration over the years decided to buy it, allegedly for £920, to preserve its architectural identity. James Lees-Milne of the National Trust disapproved of Sir Osbert's action: he felt that the classic rules of Sutton Scarsdale Hall lacked 'the picturesque gloom' of gothic ruins.

William Elmhirst, Sir Osbert's local solicitor of Hicknott and Co., Solicitors, was even more critical: his letter, dated 21st November 1946, to Sir Osbert, who was staying at 2, Carlyle Square, London, read as follows:

Dear Sir Osbert,

Re- Sutton Scarsdale

I went today to see Mr Haslam, and I went with him to inspect the above premises. I cannot really understand why you are so desirous of purchasing the Hall and the 6 acres, or thereabouts. It has no approach, it would be very expensive to develop as a building Estate and in my opinion the Hall has nothing to recommend it. It is not an ancient building and will soon become a dangerous ruin. Mr Haslam says that he is wanting to pull it down to use the stone for building houses and the bricks, which are very poor quality for crushing for the making of mortar. I told Mr Haslam that I was not in favour of purchasing it at all, but that my client was.

He said eventually that he would take £900 for it and not one penny less. I am perfectly certain it is not worth anything like £900, and, as you are desirous of buying it in your private capacity, I told Mr Haslam that I would speak to him on Monday next and give him a final answer.

I therefore should be glad if you would let me know if, in spite of what I have said, you still desire to purchase it. Further if you do, I will settle the matter on Monday on your behalf.

I am sorry to appear to disagree with you so entirely on the matter, but I have given it very careful consideration and feel that I must point this out to you.

Yours very sincerely,

W. Elmhirst

Despite this opposition Sir Osbert bought the ruins although he did not have the resources to repair the stonework and strengthen the walls as well as provide money to be used to prevent further deterioration. In his will Sir Osbert left Sutton Scarsdale Hall to his nephew, Sir Reresby Sitwell, who was also unable to provide the necessary resources, but after intense negotiations between ministries and the local authorities got the Ministry of Public Buildings and Works in 1970 to accept responsibility for the Hall: the Hall was the first Georgian ruin to receive that type of protection to ensure its future.

In 1971 Derbyshire County Council set an excellent example by agreeing to the preservation of the Hall, contributing £5,000 out of a total of £25,000 required for emergency repairs. The Ministry became English Heritage in 1984 and at the time of writing the Hall is undergoing a programme of consolidation and repair in order to make it safe for members of the public to visit and inspect. The Hall is now a Grade 1 listed building.

The two-storey stable block to Sutton Scarsdale Hall and now a Grade Two listed building comprises six cottages and the brewhouse, which was re-modelled in the 1920s to become two semi-detached dwellings.

Sutton Spring Wood

Sutton Spring Wood was possibly planted in the 17th century and since then had been a part of the Sutton Scarsdale estate until the 1919 sale. Situated about a mile to the south-west of the village of Sutton Scarsdale, it is accessed down Rock Lane from Sutton Scarsdale, as well as from Deepsic Lane which links the wood with the village of Temple Normanton.

The Arkwright family certainly used the wood as a source of timber and possibly, also, for shooting and hunting. The unsurfaced roads through the wood were for estate use and for drawing out timber. Mr Frederic Arthur Walker's report, made after an inspection on the 9th March 1921, listed the wood as being an area of 190 acres.

At the sale of the whole Sutton Scarsdale Estate, as well as a field of over 10 acres and a lodge with over two acres, over 63 acres of Sutton Spring Wood were sold to James Austin and his brother Tom Wilson Austin of Shepherdswell, Dover: the date of conveyance was 24th June 1922. On the same date of conveyance, Tom Wilson Austin and Fred Austin bought over 26 acres of Sutton Spring Wood along with Woodnook farm, which stood at the Deepsic Lane entrance to the wood.

According to Lawrence Green's historical notes on Sutton Spring Wood:

'It was then begun to be resold in plots of about 12/14 acres to be used as smallholdings. By 1924 the first residents had arrived, splitting up the plots and selling mainly to family members. The land had to be cleared at first of trees and scrub: this work was done by hand with the help of horses to pull out stumps and roots. Some of the trees, which were mainly oak, sweet chestnut and sycamore, were 3–4 feet in diameter and up to 40 feet high.

'Most of the first dwellings were caravans and railway carriages, drawn into the wood by famers' horses, as well as wooden houses, built on site in sections, most of the work being done by the owners, who were real pioneers. By the late 1940s the number of dwellings had reached about 70–80. The North East Derbyshire District Council at the time began to inspect the dwellings: several were condemned, others needed upgrading, the rest were passed as up to standard and the total number of dwellings was reduced to about 40–50. At the same time an embargo, which remains to this day, was placed on new-builds.

'At this stage Sutton Spring Wood remained an isolated community:

there were no surfaced roads, only roads for drawing out timber for estate use, no electricity, or wells to provide water sources and no main drainage system. Heating and lighting were provided by oil lamps, coal open fires and cooking ranges. To provide water, wells had to be dug by hand, some up to 30 feet deep.

Initially there was no bus service, the nearest one being at Temple Normanton, approximately a mile away. Children had to walk or cycle to school at Bonds Main or Arkwright Town. Attendance for pupils at Tupton Hall School, initially a grammar school then a large comprehensive, meant leaving home at about 7:30am, catching two buses each way and arriving home at about 5:30pm.

The wood was well-served by local businesses; a butcher called twice each week, a baker three times, newspapers and milk were available daily and groceries were ordered and delivered weekly from The Temple Normanton Co-op. Fish and hardware were also available. Eventually, Chesterfield Corporation buses ran from 6:00am, bringing newspapers for six days a week, as well as conveying parcels, until 6:00pm with a later bus at 10:00pm which ran to get people home from the picture house and theatre, both situated in Chesterfield; some buses ran to Robinson's Works.

'The bus service was very well used and, on many Saturdays, at midday, the buses would be so full that many passengers would have to get off and walk up Wray's Hill at Calow Green before the bus managed to get to the top.

'The trench for the mains water pipe was dug by the residents over one weekend; pipes were laid on the Monday and the trench filled in. Electricity was installed in 1964 when the National Coal Board needed to take a new line to Calow Green which would be directed through the wood: residents refused to agree unless the N.C.B. provided electric power to the houses. After many meetings it was agreed that electricity would be supplied with a provision that each household would pay at least £25 per year.

'The roads through the wood had been for estate use and the residents improved these by bringing red shale from the Bonds Main Colliery tip (in Temple Normanton): this was loaded by hand on to a 30 cwt. truck and then laid over many weekends; up to the present day the roads are repaired and paid for by the residents.

'For many years the residents of the wood made their own entertainment, providing whist drives and beetle drives each week; garden parties, sports days and barbecues were organised as well as teas for children on special occasions. Overall, Sutton Spring Wood was a good place to live with a happy and full life with lots of work and play. Today, Sutton Spring Wood is a good community with residents supporting each other: many of the descendants of the original families still live there.'

Epilogue

The roofless, partly demolished and ruined Sutton Scarsdale Hall still stands proudly at the top of a rise at the edge of Sutton Scarsdale village where it can be seen from many miles away; it is a continual reminder of a historic past. Many of the buildings and specific ground areas in use when the Hall was occupied still exist; for example – St Mary's Church, the brewery, now divided into two houses, the stables, converted into six cottages, Hall cellars, terrace wall, garden area, deer park containing the deer barn, archery ground, ha-ha wall, homes built to accommodate employees of the former estate, farmhouses, dog kennels, the kitchen garden across from the main Hall drive gates, parts of walls and foundation stones in the area which is now used as a car park. All houses are now privately owned.

The efforts of Harold Taylor, Sir Osbert Sitwell and Sir Reresby Sitwell have resulted in the preservation of the Hall, now a scheduled monument and Grade One listed building, maintained by and in the care of English Heritage. The part demolition of the 18th century Hall has caused the building to suffer from exposure to the elements, especially where fine plaster work still remains attached to the walls of the original entrance hall and the drawing room/ballroom above it.

At the time of writing the English Heritage maintenance programme includes conservation of the decorative plaster work, repairs to the interior walls, many of which pre-date the Hall, repairs to the stonework involving the re-pointing of mortar and the replacement of worn stones which are beyond repair, all in the interests of the safety of visitors.

Fewer farms now exist than those listed in the 1824 and 1919 auctions and they are now privately owned. Since the days of the Arkwright ownership of the estate, new individual houses and buildings have added to the overall size of the village and they continue to reflect the beauty and individuality of North East Derbyshire. However, the part-demolition of the 18th century Sutton Scarsdale Hall together with the destruction of the 19th century Sutton Rock to allow coal open casting, were undoubtedly unparalleled acts of social and architectural vandalism.

Bibliography

Anderson, P. Howard. *Forgotten Railways, the East Midlands* (David & Charles, Newton Abbot 1973)

Blythe-Lord, Robin. *A Guide to the Garden of Thorn* (Eva and John Gibson of Thorn House, Wembury Devon 2000)

Booth, Chris. *The Lancashire, Derbyshire and East Coast Railway* (Fonthill 2017)

Bradshaw, Janet. *The Church of St. Mary, Sutton Scarsdale* (Guidebook and Short History)

Bridgewater, A.N. *A History of the Adelphi Iron Works* (Duckmanton)

Bridgewater, A.N. *Coalmining on the Sutton Estates* (1994)

Bridgewater, A.N. *Arkwright Colliery, 1938-1988* (2007)

Chapman, S.D. *Stanton and Staveley: A Business History* (Woodhead-Faulkner, Cambridge 1981)

Cootes, R.J. *Britain since 1700* (Longman 1984)

Cupit, J. and Taylor, W. *The Lancashire, Derbyshire and East Coast Railway* Oakwood Press 1984

Downes-Rose, G. *What was Here, before Arkwright Town?* (1992)

Downes-Rose, G. *Arkwrights' Railway* (1992)

Downes-Rose, G. *Duckmanton Moor, Its Land, Industries and People* (1993)

Downes-Rose, G. *A History of Duckmanton Moor* (1993)

Downes-Rose, G. *Arkwright Town, Two Local Brooks* (1994)

Downes-Rose, G. *Coal Mining: A Personal Perspective* (2000)

Evans, Sian. *Life below Stairs in the Victorian and Edwardian Country House* (The National Trust 2011)

Fitton, R.S. *The Arkwrights, Spinners of Fortune* (Manchester University Press 1989)

Gladwin, D. *Diary of events in Derbyshire, 1852-5* (Chesterfield Local History Library)

Gomme, Andor. *Smith of Warwick* (Shaun Tyas, Stamford 2000)

Harris, Alexandra. *Romantic Moderns* (Thames and Hudson 2010)

Hey, David. *Derbyshire: A History* (Carnegie Publishing 2008)

Hodgkins, David, ed. *The Records of The Cromford and High Peak Railway Company* (Derbyshire Record Society Vol. XXXII 2008)

Kettle, Pamela. *Sutton Scarsdale's Story Part 1: The Leekes of Sutton* (Morley's Bible and Book Shop Limited 1988)

Kettle, Pamela and Ryden. Philip. *Sutton cum Duckmanton Parish Registry, 1662–1837* (Derbyshire Record Society Vol. XV111 1992)

Kettle, Pamela. *Parsons of Sutton cum Duckmanton* (the author, Sutton Scarsdale 1995)

Kettle, Pamela. *The History of the Sutton cum Duckmanton Endowed School, 1693-1936* (1996)

Kettle, Pamela. *Oldcotes: The last Mansion built by Bess of Hardwick* (Merton Priory Press 2000)

Kingscott, G. *Lost Railways of Derbyshire* (Countryside Books 2007)

Lees-Milne, James. *The Batchelor Duke* (John Murray 1991)

Musson, Jeremy. *Up and Down Stairs: The History of The Country House Servant* (John Murray 2009)

Porter, Lindsey. *Duchess Georgiana: Georgian Britain's Most Popular Woman: A New Study.* (Guideline Books and Sales 2015)

Robinson, P. *The Smiths of Chesterfield - A History of the Griffin Foundry, Brampton, 1775-1833*

Sheppard, Richard. *Sutton Scarsdale Hall, Derbyshire* (Trent and Peak Archeological Trust, R. Sheppard, 1996)

Sitwell, Osbert. *Left Hand, Right Hand* (Macmillan & Co. Ltd. 1945)

Sitwell, Sacheverell. *British Architects and Craftsmen* (B.T. Batsford 1948)

Spalding, Frances. *John Piper, Myfanwy Piper, Lives in Art* (Oxford University Press 2009)

Turbutt, Gladwyn. *A History of Derbyshire* (Merton Priory Press, 1999)

Warwick, Sarah. *Upstairs and Downstairs* (SevenOaks 2011)

Wilmot, David. *The Lancashire Derbyshire and East Coast Railway* (2002)

Winter, John. Edwards, David. Knight, Kev. *Wingerworth Hall's American Connections* (Wings Magazine 2017)

Ziegler Philip. *Osbert Sitwell* (Chatto and Windus 1998)

The following three documents were used by permission of the Duke of Devonshire and the Chatsworth House Trust:

1. Frances Arkwright's Journal, 1844
2. Frances Arkwright's Words of Songs
3. Letters of Response to 1849 lithograph of Frances Arkwright

Acknowledgements

I would like to thank all those who have helped in many different ways my research in the writing of this book; without their help and support it would not have been possible.

Firstly, I would like to thank His Grace the 12th Duke of Devonshire and the Chatsworth House Trust for the provision of journals relating to the Arkwright family and initially possessed by the 6th Duke of Devonshire; also archivists and librarians Andrew Peppitt (now retired) and James Towe, also use of the 1849 lithograph of Frances Arkwright commissioned by the 6th Duke. With thanks also to Chesterfield Local History Library and the Matlock Public Record Office.

Mary Ravey, Madge Coupe, Betty Hopkinson, Roger Glazebrook and Maxwell Craven for giving me initial advice and information regarding the estate; the Philadelphia Museum of Art, *Country Life*, Michael Smart, Stuart Pollard, Susan Crowley and Vic Halksworth for providing me with various photographs; Susan Watts, grand-daughter of Captain Penrose, for providing photographs as well as her mother Ruth's written memories of living at Sutton Rock; Faye Hall, for providing me with her mother Wendie's written and spoken memories of living on Rock Lane; Tom and Peter Arkwright's family history research material with the kind permission of Mrs Tom Arkwright; Darrell Clarke for information on the Arkwright family, the recording of the lead plate and the gift of books; Chris Beevers, archivist at Renishaw Hall, for information on the Arkwrights via the Renishaw Hall archives and Mrs Alexandra Hayward for a reproduction of John Piper's painting of Sutton Scarsdale Hall; Barbara and Len Barber, for providing photographs, original letters, documents etc. including research material from the late Pamela Kettle's collection; Robin Blythe-Lord for information on 'Thorn' and William Arkwright; Roy Slack, John Coulson and Gordon Hill for conversations regarding Sutton Scarsdale Hall and knowledgeable tours of the Hall and surrounding land; David Allen of Wm. Twigg of Matlock; Lawrence Green for his notes on Sutton Spring Wood; Ann and Zoe Penrose for photographs and a DVD of Captain Penrose and his family; David and Ann Sewell for photographs and information from *Derbyshire Life* articles; Richard Sheppard for permission to use his written history of Sutton Scarsdale Hall, a report for English Heritage; Dr Robert Houlton for recording my first tour of Sutton Scarsdale Hall for the Arkwright Society in 2006 which resulted in an audio CD of the tour being produced: the CD became the main impetus in the writing of my book.

I would also like to thank Tom Blyth of Bannister Publications Ltd for his help, expert advice and for the patience he has shown in the preparation of this book.

Photographs

1. Robert Arkwright
2. North front of the Hall (Nadin's Series)
3. Hall entrance drive and gates
4. East front of the Hall (Nadin's Series)
5. West front of the Hall (servant entrance) (Nadin's Series)
6. St. Mary's Church, Sutton Scarsdale.
7. The gardens, Sutton Scarsdale Hall (Nadin's Series)
8. The gardens, Sutton Scarsdale Hall (Nadin's Series)
9. Lady, possibly a member of the Arkwright family at the entrance to the Hall drive.
10. Gardeners at west front of Hall (Nadin's Series)
11. Frances Crawford Arkwright, nee Kemble
12. J.P.Neale's drawing of Sutton Scarsdale Hall
13. Entrance Hall (Country Life Picture Library)
14. 'Best Staircase' (Country Life Picture Library)
15. Invitation card to William Arkwright's 21st birthday celebrations
16. Arkwright's 'clotted cream container'
17. Bolsover Station
18. South front of the Hall next to the church
19. Farmers/tenants, probably taken on rent collection day: date unknown
20. The Station Hotel, Arkwright Town
21. Market Place Station (L.D. & E.C. Railway)
22. Arkwright Town Station
23. Staff at Sutton Scarsdale Hall, 1903
24. Staff at Sutton Scarsdale Hall. Date unknown, but possibly early 20th century
25. Sutton Rock (Nadin's Series)

26. Charles Cockburn , a former resident of Sutton Rock
27. Church adjacent to east front of Hall
28. Hall stables
29. East front of Sutton Scarsdale Hall, painting by Daniel Halksworth.
30. West front of Sutton Scarsdale Hall, painting by John Piper.
31. Terrace wall from rear gardens of Palterton Lane
32. Sutton Scarsdale Hall in its current state (east and north fronts)
33. Sutton Scarsdale Hall in its current state (east front)
34. The Hall Pine Room reconstructed and used in the 1945 film *Kitty*
35. The Hall Pine Room reconstructed and used in the 1945 film *Kitty*
36. The Hall Pine Room reconstructed and used in the 1945 film *Kitty*
37. Image of re-constructed first Oak Room (Philadelphia Museum of Art)
38. Image of re-constructed second Oak Room (Philadelphia Museum of Art)
39. Lithograph of Frances Arkwright, ordered by the 6th Duke on her death in 1849 (by permission of The Duke of Devonshire and The Chatsworth House Trust)
40. William Arkwright
41. Agnes Arkwright
42. Pointer dog outside Thorn House